I0817000

"We are always at the beginning of things,
in the fragile moment that holds the power of life.
We are always at the morning of the world."

FRANÇOIS CHENG

Under the Sign of the Moon

MAURO COLAGRECO
MIRAZUR

TEXT **LAURA COLAGRECO**
PHOTOGRAPHS BY **MATTEO CARASSALE**
FOREWORD **VANDANA SHIVA**

ABRAMS / NEW YORK

FOREWORD

MIRAZUR: THE RESTAURANT IN THE GARDEN

We are members of the Earth family in a garden of biodiversity. Food is the currency that flows from the soil, through the plants—their roots, leaves, flowers, fruits—through our kitchens, to our gut microbiome.

We are what we eat.

We are the soil humus. Humus shapes humanity. Humus grows life. Humus and living soil grow flavors, taste, health, nutrition.

We are the nutrition and breath the plants give us as food and oxygen.

We are the biodiversity we grow and eat. The biodiversity of the soil, the plants in our garden, and our gut is an interconnected flow of life and nourishment, of taste and beauty. The richer the biodiversity in the living soil, the richer the phytochemicals, trace elements, and nutrients in our food, the tastier our food.

Nature knows no waste. Nature does not create monocultures. Nature does not create one-dimensional plants. The web of life is a food web. Soil grows plants, plants and organic matter grow soil. We used to eat 10,000 different varieties of plant life. Now our diet is reduced to a few dozen globally traded commodities, empty of taste and nutrition and full of toxins. Mirazur reconnects our food to biodiversity; the diversity not just of plants, but of the different parts of plants— the roots, the leaves, the flowers, the fruits.

Mirazur makes the act of eating a rich conversation with the cosmos, with all living beings in the garden, the soil, the biodiversity of plants and insects, the farmers who grew the food, the cooks who transformed it.

Our senses are not a distraction in a mechanistic Cartesian world reduced to measurement and quantity. They are our communication with the elements in all their diverse forms—the earth, water, breath, fire, space. We are made of the same elements that the earth and universe are made of. When we eat food grown and cooked with love, care, and consciousness, it raises our awareness of being part of the living earth. Our urge to care for the earth expands to include all life. We are no longer thoughtless, careless consumers. We become citizens of the Earth—Earth beings.

Mirazur invites you to open your palates, hearts, and minds to the amazing garden of biodiversity we can grow wherever we are.

Let us regenerate gardens of hope and love.

Vandana Shiva

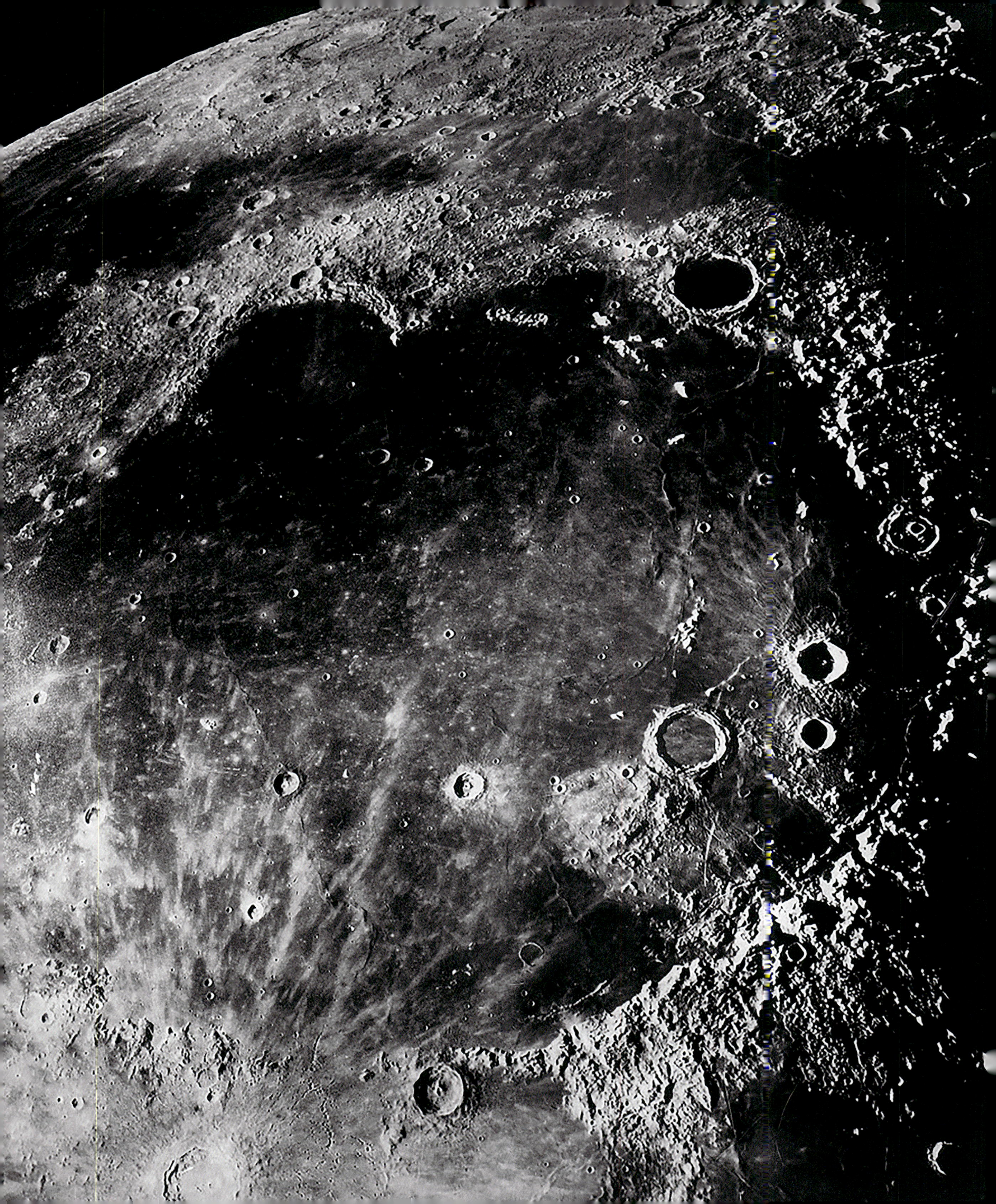

CONTENTS

5
FOREWORD

9
INTRODUCTION

EARTH — 27
ROOTS

WATER — 71
LEAVES

AIR — 113
FLOWERS

FIRE — 159
FRUITS

201
LUNAR MENU

283
LIQUIDS

285
DRINKS

INTRODUCTION

"You will find something more in woods than in books. Trees and stones will teach you that which you can never learn from masters."

Saint Bernard de Clairvaux

A profession is a passion, but also a skill that is acquired over time, as we enter into a dialogue with what we love.

It is an experience that opens us up to the world, transforms us, and enters us into a flow that is very close to the natural movement of life. It is a dialogue that, at Mirazur, is expressed in a singular language, immersed in the Mediterranean landscape and permeated by all the sonorities of nature.

In this unique enclave between France and Italy, Mirazur embodies a sort of multidimensional border dialect, enriched by different origins and multiple influences.

It is a language created by the synergy between the kitchen and the landscape, between cooking pots and gardening, and that continues to reinvent itself, offering us new revelations.

It is a form of communication that summons all the senses and that results in an increasingly precise sensitivity, refined by the beauty of the world and the joy of sharing.

Working the soil is a chance to get in touch with the substance of cooking, to tune into its deepest heartbeat.

Cooking is, above all, about "translating" a landscape and, by means of food, giving people the opportunity to incorporate it, to make it their own.

It is about planting landscapes in minds to connect cooking to the earth, to return to the spiral that, crossing boundaries of time and space, makes "humus" the substance of our "humanity."

Gardener and cook: both are professions that involve transmission, passion, deciphering signs, enchanting the world.

Cooking and gardening: two breaths in the same action of breathing.

GARDENS WITH A RESTAURANT

"Gardens are artworks that escape the control of their makers."

Abderrazak Benchaabane

Having a garden means you can enjoy an open-air taste laboratory. For a restaurant, this is a tremendous chance, and the ideal opportunity to embark on a process of exploration. The different stages in the ripening of a fruit, the evolution of a flower or a leaf, the daily micro-transformations of plants and landscapes: everything is revealed in a tangible way that not only extends the range of culinary possibilities but also hones our perception and senses. Mirazur's evolution is inextricably linked to that of its gardens. A horticultural project that has developed over the years now takes the form of five gardens, grouped together as the "Sanctuaires du Mirazur," a name chosen to reflect our desire to create spaces of conservation and biodiversity, places where the preciousness of life is celebrated in all its manifestations.

Is Mirazur a restaurant with a garden, or is it a multifaceted garden with a restaurant?

From the first green space below Mirazur, with its Menton lemon trees, its aromatic herbs, and the exuberance of its ornamental trees and plants, to the wilder plot of land in Castillon, in the mountains north of Menton, Mirazur's different gardens bear witness to a fertile commitment that has been sustained since the restaurant opened in 2006. This venture is in keeping with the history of the restaurant's location, as Mirazur stands in the former gardens of the splendid Villa Maria Serena, whose owner decided to bequeath a portion of its land to his gardener. Its evolution honors the essence of the place.

The Romans believed that every space is inhabited by a *genius loci*, a minor divinity that protects its singularity. Settling in a place, building there, involved communicating with the god, negotiating for him to stay. For them, living in a world devoid of spirit, and therefore of meaning, implied danger.

Mirazur poetically inhabits a region whose beauty and rich produce provide the necessary ingredients to create the ultimate dining experience. Places that are at the heart of inspiration and wonder are shared in the experience of guests at the restaurant. Conscientious work with the soil and the land causes us to reexamine the way we see our profession and to try to restore to gastronomy its meaning, depth, and richness.

How did the knowledge acquired by culinary students become so disconnected from the origin of products and the cycles of nature?

In Ancient Greece, a cook's training involved studying the Earth and cosmic interactions. To create a recipe, understanding the movement of the tides and stars was as important as learning culinary techniques.

Throughout the world, since the dawn of time, different civilizations have fed their imagination with stories celebrating the cyclical character of nature and the importance of respecting the balance of the universal order. Drawing their first inspiration from this mythology, the different facets of their lives reflected this attachment to the cosmos.

The disconnection we experience from our environments is a relatively recent phenomenon. Its impact on the damage to our ecosystems has become increasingly evident, as has the need to act to halt this.

This became abundantly clear during the pandemic, when we experienced on a global scale the extent to which separation from our environments makes us fragile and dependent. We became aware of the importance of strengthening our local and community ties and of the need to nurture our close relationships to ensure our survival. And we all witnessed the way in which nature regained momentum with the decrease of our activities.

THE VIRTUOUS CYCLE

"I carved these words into the wood of one of the mountain huts:
'Good diet, good deeds, good conscience.' These three things are inseparable.
If one is missing, none will be achieved. If one is achieved, the others will be, too."

Masanobu Fukuoka

There are things we read that change our lives and reveal to us universes that were previously hidden from us. These are true encounters—books that give us fresh momentum and move us in a new direction. They will always hold a special place in the library of our hearts.

The One Straw Revolution is one such book. It was written in 1975 by the farmer and microbiologist Masanobu Fukuoka (1913–2008), who sowed the seeds of what is known as "natural" farming, and provided food for thought for the creators of permaculture, the ecologists Bill Mollison and David Holmgren. Reading his work has served as the most vital fertilizer for the growth of our gardens. Analyzing the life forces present in the area, providing necessary protection for the soils, and saving resources in order to make systems more autonomous and efficient have been among the most useful lessons we have learned.

More than simply a way of gardening, permaculture is a philosophy that is not limited to a vegetable garden but establishes a balanced and respectful relationship between humans and nature. It encourages us to observe and invites us to discover the wisdom that is inherent in all living things.

The study of permaculture and its application in our gardens has opened us up to a richer dialogue with those around us and has led to new and beneficial encounters. We have invited people who inspire us, participated in events that help us reflect together, and joined groups and institutions committed to the same values, in order to forge ever-stronger connections around the care of the land, the protection of farmers' seeds, and the cultivation of biodiversity.

We have established an internal schedule to enable front-of-house and kitchen staff to spend time in the gardens. This way of functioning, which is rooted in circularity, gives everyone hands-on experience working alongside the gardeners and provides an understanding of the connection between creativity in the kitchen, the dining experience, the treatment of waste, and work in the garden.

For most of those involved, this is the first time that such an activity has been offered as part of their work routine in a restaurant. Some of them discover a new passion, and, for everyone, it is the chance to learn and to share the enjoyment and the experience of being in direct contact with the soil.

This training enables the teams to develop a global vision of what defines Mirazur's universe, so that they can instill it in their day-to-day work and in the way they present the restaurant and its dishes to guests. It is an invitation to participate in the creation of virtuous cycles in our locale and, in doing so, to contribute to the beauty of the world.

FROM THE EARTH TO THE STARS

"The stars are like letters that inscribe themselves at every moment in the sky. Everything in the world is full of signs. All events are coordinated."

Plotinus, *Enneads*

Everything begins in the earth. This assertion, both powerful and poetic, is a leitmotiv of permaculture and all practices that favour sustainable agriculture. Understanding the structure and fundamental role of soils in the health of ecosystems provides a surprising insight into the power of the infinitely small and the impact of interdependence. Beneath our feet, veritable societies of living organisms are growing, interacting, and forming a framework that is essential to the expansion of life.

These practices, which aim to improve the soil structure of our gardens, dig our roots more deeply into the land. Enriching the soils, preparing them to welcome and nourish the different plant species, and making compost—to return to the cycle of life a large part of the waste generated in our kitchens—have given us a better understanding of the uniqueness of each living organism and the interactions it produces.

We have understood that the way life works is all about cooperation. We have gained a broader perspective, and biodynamics has entered into a natural dialogue with us in our gardens. It was the wonderful work of a winemaker friend, Aris Blancardi, of the Selvadolce vineyard in Bordighera (Italy), that introduced us to this approach to agriculture.

An encounter that opened the door to new understanding, and encouraged us, like the people of Antiquity, to study the sky to work the earth.

An enchanting philosophy that perceives the Earth as a living organism open to cosmic influences.

A vision that commends contemplation and the subtle forces at work in nature and in our lives.

An ode to life that aligns us with vast cosmic exchanges and knits us into the great fabric of the Universe.

THE MOVEMENT OF LIFE

"Towards evening, abandon yourself to your double destiny:
live in the heart of the landscape and wave to the shooting stars."

François Cheng

Biodynamics shows us the Earth as a complex, self-regulating system in which living organisms have a synergetic relationship to their environment, the atmosphere, and the stars. This agricultural system was conceived in 1924 by the philosopher Rudolf Steiner (1861–1925) to address the concerns of German farmers faced with problems related to the use of chemical products and the advance of industrial farming. Central to its approach are practices such as the synchronization of lunar and crop calendars and the use of products based on medicinal plants, cow manure, and quartz.

The complex biodynamic calendar divides the year into days that are favorable or unfavorable for different aspects of agricultural labor. These divisions are defined by the movement of the Moon around planet Earth and by its passages through the twelve constellations of the zodiac. It was developed more than fifty years ago by the German farmer and researcher Maria Thun (1922–2012), who was a disciple of Rudolf Steiner and an admirer of his work. She established the correlations between the growth of plants and lunar cycles based on extensive observations. She noted the influence of beneficial cosmic stimuli that act directly on the development of roots, leaves, flowers, and fruits, and thus created a calendar in which four "formative forces" are attributed to different parts of the plants: earth for roots, water for leaves, air for flowers, and fire for fruits.

We have analyzed this biodynamic lunar calendar and begun to apply the principles to organize the timing of tasks in our gardens. Our desire is to stay open-minded, and so our approach is one of continual exploration rather than adherence to a dogma. We keep an eye on the lunar calendar, and our five senses on the ground.

THE GREAT PAUSE

"There is nothing you can see that is not a flower;
there is nothing you can think that is not the Moon."

Matsuo Bashô

How does the starry sky we see at night affect living things? Are we connected to the stars? What effect does the Moon have? Is there another energy that gives cohesion to everything that exists?

Such questions have spanned the ages and civilizations and have inspired very varied representations of calendars engraved on stones, animal bones, and clay tablets.

Our relationship to the sky and the cosmos permeates the founding principles of biodynamics. It is infused by the invitation to observe all the tiny changes that take place in nature through the influence of the movement of the stars. It is a view that makes us aware of subtle forces and requires an openness to tackling notions that have become too vague. In our globalized lives, we are not sufficiently observant, not sufficiently precise, and so we deny these influences.

The period of quarantine created a time for us to retreat, to reflect, to get in touch with silence, and to observe nature. At a time when the pandemic was highlighting concerns about our food systems, we had the time and the open-mindedness needed to deepen our ties with the Earth and to become aware of the tremendous collective dimension that exists in nature.

In our study of life forces, we have noticed that all living things work together: each plant, each insect, each bird. And this realization was a precious source of inspiration during that long and difficult period. We noted how, in the world today, we have lost the ability to perceive the wonders of existence. And so we miss out on the simple joys that everyday life has to offer us, the treasures that nature presents us with.

Acknowledging the life within us and rediscovering the richness of the world has become a need, and the driving force behind our desire to continue moving forward.

THE FOUR UNIVERSES

"Happiness is a little thing that you nibble on, sitting on the ground, in the sun."

Jean Giraudoux

One day, in the middle of lockdown, the spark of an idea formed: when we reopened our restaurant, we would share with our guests the admiration we feel for all these explorations by introducing into our cuisine the lunar calendar used to plan the work in our gardens. We would cook according to the rhythm of the stars and offer, during this most unusual spring of our lives, the fragrance of our gratitude to the Earth.

It would be a tribute to this mysterious intelligence that runs through all living beings and to our life companions on this planet, without whom we would not be able to live on it. It would be a totally new, all-encompassing experience that would raise awareness of the connections between the structure of living organisms and that of the cosmos. A journey into the special energy of each day, through a menu conceived in accordance with the fluctuations of the biodynamic calendar.

Under the sign of the Moon, we decided to offer four different universes, with, as their central themes, roots, leaves, flowers, and fruits—the four parts of plants represented in the lunar calendar to mark the days when energy is most concentrated.

An inspiration that follows the movement of the Moon in the sky and its passage through the twelve constellations of the zodiac, each belonging to an element of nature, the inspiration matrix of the lunar calendar linking roots to the earth, leaves to water, flowers to air, and fruits to fire.

This calendar, created over years of research, is based on the following observations:

– Root crops are best planted when the Moon is passing through the constellations associated with the earth: Taurus, Virgo, Capricorn;

– Leafy plants proliferate when the Moon is associated with the water signs: Cancer, Scorpio, Pisces;

– Floral plants combine particularly well with the air signs: Gemini, Libra, Aquarius;

– Fruits grow best with the fire signs: Aries, Leo, Sagittarius.

After this time of compulsory confinement, we realized how much people need to get out into the open air, to get closer to the earth, and to cultivate a special awareness of the wonder of other living beings. So we decided, during this first period, to move out into our gardens to offer our guests tapas in the form of a picnic under the lemon trees below the restaurant. We changed the decoration of the tables and of the restaurant: since that time, it has taken on the look of each theme and is transformed with the rotation of the four universes, to promote a complete sensory immersion.

We offer visits to our Rosmarino vegetable garden, just a stone's throw from the restaurant, on the iconic Boulevard de Garavan, which are led by our gardeners and restaurant staff.

It gives us great joy to note the growing interest of our guests in these visits, and we are continually surprised by it. It is a great opportunity to showcase the work carried out in our gardens and to talk about our connection with the Earth. To share, finally, the unique natural and cultural heritage of our surroundings and the expression of a continuing quest for freedom that is manifested in a bold and fresh approach to the creation of the gastronomic experience.

KOHLRABI AND SHELLFISH page 203

CARROT, KUMQUAT, AND PORK BELLY TERRINE page 204

WASABI AND GREEN APPLE page 206

"In the darkness of our garden soils, rootlets and radicles, rhizomes and tubers spread out in a variety of shapes, colors, textures, and behaviors."

MENTON ONION, CARAMOTE SHRIMP, AND RED SHISO page 207

NEW POTATO RAGOUT page 209

FISH, **LICORICE**, AND **BLACK GARLIC** page 210

TURMERIC AND APRICOT page 211

“It is the light falling continually from heaven which alone gives a tree the energy to send powerful roots deep into the earth. The tree is really rooted in the sky.”

Simone Weil, *Human Personality*

BEET AND CAVIAR page 212

GINGER AND PENJA WHITE PEPPER page 216

ONION AND COMTÉ CUBE page 218

ASSORTED **RADISH**, FISH, AND CITRUS FRUIT ROSETTE page 219

FISH OF THE DAY AND **LEEKS** page 220

LEAVES

WATER

THE UNIVERSE OF LEAVES

"With time and patience, the mulberry leaf becomes satiny."

Chinese proverb

The lunar calendar associates the universe of leaves with the element of water and the passage of the Moon through the constellations of the zodiac signs belonging to this element: Cancer, Scorpio, and Pisces. The rise of sap in plants is linked to this cosmic movement and to the particular configuration of the Moon and planets during these phases. In our gardens, salad leaves are grown during "leaf days." Should they happen to be planted on a "root day," lettuces will be smaller and have denser heads.

With their multitude of shapes and textures, leaves help us appreciate the surprising diversity that exists in nature. Seeing a plant emerge and grow, watching its stems grow upward and its leaves unfurl, we are able to witness the precise and precious movement of the plant from earth to sky. In this dance, water present in the leaves resonates with the movement of the waves of the Mediterranean, which lap our land borders.

Among the tasks most often associated with leaves in our gardens are the treatments that we use to prevent or cure certain diseases: liquid manure and plant-based preparations, applied at very precise moments and by hand, in the form of sprays. Among the plants most often used in liquid manure, we find nettles—very nutritive with their abundance of minerals—which provide lots of nitrogen and improve the process of photosynthesis in the leaves; horsetail, which supplies silica to strengthen the plant's structure and, like garlic-based preparations, prevents diseases associated with fungal growth; and comfrey, rich in potassium, which delays leaf senescence and, when added to compost, helps speed up its transformation. Olive-oil-based soap and neem oil are applied occasionally to repel insects, aphids, red spiders, and other small bugs associated with leaf diseases.

In addition to growing plants in our gardens, we have been studying the wild varieties present in our region for several years. We have foraged and researched from the start, but over the last few years, we have intensified these activities, and a gastronomic ethnobotanist and an archeologist–anthropologist have joined our team at Mirazur's research and development center. We have identified plant species that not only are interesting in terms of being edible, but that also play a part in enriching biodiversity and the balance of ecosystems. These plants, which include the different types of Chenopodium, commonly known as goosefoot, have endured through the ages and have proved themselves to be very versatile and well-adapted to the extremely dry and hot conditions. In our gardens, we have laid out a space for replanting these "wild" species, with the aim of cultivating them, exploring their culinary uses, and helping both to promote and conserve them.

The season of spring, with its freshness and verdant eruption of leaves and subtle textures, is a high point for using leaves in the kitchen. During the summer, the strength of the Mediterranean sun, more favorable to ripening fruits, will have a direct impact on leaves, conferring on them other—different but no less interesting—qualities. In spring and in summer, we grow rhubarb, celtuce, New Zealand spinach, different varieties of lettuce, salad burnet, chickweed, shiso, Malabar spinach, and fennel, while in autumn and winter, different varieties of kale, cabbage, radicchio, red Belgian endive, and winter lettuces find their place in our gardens.

CELTUCE, STRACCIATELLA, AND CAVIAR page 223

GARDEN SALAD AND VERMOUTH SAUCE page 224

GREEN TEA AND BABY SQUID page 225

FENNEL, VANILLA, AND WHITE CHOCOLATE page 226

MALABAR SPINACH AND FISH TARTARE page 227

"Plants have never abandoned the sea: rather they have brought it where it did not exist. They have transformed the universe into an immense atmospheric sea and have transmitted their marine habits to all other beings. Photosynthesis is, in this sense, a cosmic process of fluidification of the universe ..."

Emanuele Coccia, *The Life of Plants*

NEW ZEALAND SPINACH AND SQUID page 228

FISH OF THE DAY AND **SHISO** page 229

DULSE SEAWEED AND CHERRIES page 230

"Seeing a plant emerge and grow, watching its stems grow upward and its leaves unfurl, we are able to witness the precise and precious movement of the plant from earth to sky. In this dance, water present in the leaves resonates with the movement of the waves of the Mediterranean, which lap our land."

OYSTER AND **CODIUM** page 232

LAMB **MILLEFEUILLE** page 234

MATE AND WHITE CHOCOLATE page 235

OXALIS AND CRAB page 237

RED BELGIAN ENDIVE AND BLEU DU QUEYRAS SAUCE page 238

RADICCHIO RAVIOLI AND WILD BOAR CONSOMMÉ page 239

CHOCOLATE AND **ROSEMARY** page 240

FLOWERS

AIR

THE UNIVERSE OF FLOWERS

"Each year, through its flower, [the tree] asks heaven for a fruit."

Paul Claudel

In the movement transmitted by the variations in the lunar calendar, "flower days" correspond to the position of the Moon in the constellations belonging to the element of air: Gemini, Libra, and Aquarius.

Inextricably linked with spring, the exhilaration of colors, the intoxication of fragrances, and the declaration of love, flowers are the parts of plants that best convey the notions of transience and subtlety.

Menton is one of Alpes-Maritimes' "Villes et Villages Fleuris" (Towns and Villages in Bloom), a land that inspired botanists, who came here to cultivate exotic gardens and who left traces of the Belle Époque on its landscapes. The flowerbeds overflowing with bougainvilleas, jasmines, and roses, the blossoming of wisteria and palm trees, and the delicate beauty of jacarandas give this town an undeniable charm.

It is primarily flowers that open our eyes to the exchanges that take place between plants through the air, and especially their connection with the marvelous world of insects and other pollinators. They provide a floral covering to the plant's sexual organs and enable its reproduction. This occurs by air and is assisted, in most cases, by the activity of insects: more than eighty percent of floral plants are pollinated by insects, such as bees and bumblebees.

These pollinators play a vital role in balancing ecosystems: they are highly sensitive "bioindicators" that enable us to assess the health of an environment. Considered as "little suns" by Rudolf Steiner, bees have a fundamental part to play in a biodynamic garden. We have discovered the benefits of beekeeping and of honey in the human diet, and our gardeners have been taught how to maintain beehives in our gardens. These beehives are designed to encourage the pollinization process, to contribute to the biodiversity of endemic honey bees, such as the Ligurian bee, and to maintain environmental balance. The aim is not to obtain honey, but what is harvested is used in the restaurant as a precious elixir from our gardens.

The sense of luxury and privilege associated with the notion of transience stems largely from direct contact with the cycles of flowers, which encourage us to pay attention to subtle details and to the passing of time.

In our gardens, boron- and copper-based homeopathic treatments are applied to plants during the waxing phase of the moon to encourage their growth.

The season with the fewest flowers is winter. This is the chance for us to explore rarer, more exotic flowers, whose growth is favored by Menton's microclimate and that surprise our senses with new flavors and aromas. It is also the time to work with dried flowers and with floral preserves that we prepared earlier in the year: rose, jasmine, elderflower, acacia, linden. And at the end of winter, we celebrate our almond trees, the first fruit trees to flower and to give our dishes a foretaste of spring.

We take advantage of early springtime to serve our guests the first wild violets, picked in the mountains, and nasturtiums, which grow all over the place in our gardens. Then, it is the turn of the fresh, tender petals of the little white roses that bloom in May and of other—more colorful and larger—rose varieties that appear in the month of June. In summer, we need to find other types of flowers, with more marked, animal notes, like those of aromatic plants, such as lavender and rosemary. This inspires us to explore and experiment, as has been the case with the yucca and banana tree flowers in our garden, which we started using when we introduced our lunar menu.

Flowers have always been a signature of Mirazur cuisine—an affinity that revives a tradition dating back to Antiquity and to the different civilizations throughout the ages that have served flowers on their menus. This is why our gardens are full of flowers: in addition to those already mentioned and those borne by vegetables, aromatic herbs, and trees—arugula (rocket), savory, thyme, garlic, sage, almond, Judas tree—we grow yarrows, chrysanthemums, cosmos, marigolds, dahlias, mallows, sunflowers, flax, hollyhocks, and, in the mountains, saffron. Pollen and honey are also associated with the universe of flowers to evoke the importance of the link between flowers and their pollinators.

ROSE TUILES AND SMOKED MACKEREL page 242

CHRYSANTHEMUM DOME, FLAKED CRAB, AND SPRING FLOWERS page 243

PETITS POIS AND **ELDERFLOWER** RAGOUT page 244

NASTURTIUM FLOWER AND CUCUMBER page 245

"The sense of luxury and privilege associated with the notion of transience stems largely from direct contact with the cycles of flowers, which encourage us to pay attention to subtle details and to the passing of time."

COSMOS VEIL AND VEAL TARTARE page 246

SUNFLOWER RAVIOLI AND PARMESAN BOUILLON page 247

ZUCCHINI FLOWER RAVIOLI AND CHICKEN CONSOMMÉ page 248

POLLEN, HONEY, AND PROPOLIS page 249

HIBISCUS AND BEET ROSE page 250

LOBSTER AND **VANILLA** page 251

ARTICHOKE TART page 252

YUCCA AND GRAPEFRUIT page 253

"Our relationship to the sky and the cosmos permeates the founding principles of biodynamics. It is infused by the invitation to observe all the tiny changes that take place in nature through the influence of the movement of the stars."

BORAGE FLOWERS AND RAZOR CLAMS page 254

OSMANTHUS, LANGOUSTINE, AND GREEN APPLE page 255

“An enchanting philosophy that perceives the Earth as a living organism open to cosmic influences.

A vision that commends contemplation and the subtle forces at work in nature and in our lives.

An ode to life that aligns us with vast cosmic exchanges and knits us into the great fabric of the Universe.”

SAFFRON AND MUSSELS page 257

VIOLET AND UNPASTEURIZED GOAT MILK page 258

CAESAR'S MUSHROOM TARTARE page 261

"The different stages in the ripening of a fruit, the evolution of a flower or a leaf, the daily micro-transformations of plants and landscapes: everything is revealed in a tangible way that not only extendes the range of culinary possibilities but also hones our perception and senses."

RED AND WHITE **STRAWBERRIES** AND FOIE GRAS page 262

TAGGIASCA OLIVE AND LEMON page 263

ZUCCHINI, EGGPLANT, AND **TOMATO** TART page 268

RASPBERRIES AND VERBENA page 269

BUTTERNUT SQUASH AND FISH TARTARE page 270

FOIE GRAS AND **PORCINI MUSHROOMS** FROM THE COL DE TENDE page 271

MALLARD AND **QUINCE** TERRINE page 272

PRICKLY PEAR AND YUZU page 274

CHIA, **CITRON**, AND VENISON TARTARE page 275

FISH OF THE DAY AND **SUDACHI** SAUCE page 275

SQUAB AND **BANANA FROM THE GARDEN** page 276

MENTON LEMON AND STRACCIATELLA page 278

LUNAR MENU

TURNIP AND SHELLFISH TARTLET

SERVES 4

FOR THE TARTLET PASTRY
3/4 cup + 1 tbsp. (3 1/2 oz./100 g) pastry (soft) flour
1 tbsp. (15 g) softened butter
1 tbsp. sunflower oil
1 3/4 oz. (50 g) egg white
1/2 tsp. (3 g) salt

FOR THE TURNIP VEIL
1 turnip
7/8 cup (200 ml) water

FOR THE PICKLED TURNIP CUBES
1 turnip
1 cup (240 ml) cider vinegar
1/3 cup + 1 1/2 tbsp. (100 ml) water
1/2 cup (3 1/2 oz./100 g) superfine (caster) sugar
2 tbsp. (25 g) unrefined sea salt

FOR THE FILLING
4 1/4 oz. (120 g) cooked lobster claw meat
Scant 1/4 cup (1 3/4 oz./50 g) trout roe
3/4 oz. (20 g) pickled turnip cubes
1 1/2 tbsp. (25 ml) crème fraîche
1 tbsp. (3 g) snipped chives
1 tsp. (3 g) finely chopped shallot
2 tsp. yuzu juice
Salt

FOR THE YUZU GEL
2 1/2 tbsp. (1 oz./30 g) superfine (caster) sugar
1 cup + 1 tbsp. (250 ml) water
1/2 cup (125 ml) yuzu juice
4 tsp. (1/4 oz./8 g) agar-agar powder

TO SERVE
Chives

FOR THE TARTLET PASTRY

Preheat the oven to 340°F (170°C/gas 4). Mix the flour, softened butter, and sunflower oil in a stand mixer fitted with the hook attachment. When the dough begins to come together, add the egg white and salt. Continue mixing until the dough comes away from the sides of the bowl. Be careful not to overmix it: the dough should not get hot. Cover and let rest in the refrigerator for at least 1 hour. Roll out the dough (pastry) to 1/8 in. (3 mm) thick and use to line four 3 in. (8 cm) diameter tartlet pans. Press on top with another pan, then cut off the excess dough using a small knife. Bake blind in the oven for 10 minutes.

FOR THE TURNIP VEIL

Using a mandoline, cut the turnip into very thin (2 mm) slices. Cut into petals using a cookie (pastry) cutter. Set aside in a bowl of water.

FOR THE PICKLED TURNIP CUBES

Peel the turnip, dice into 1/4 in. (5 mm) cubes, and place in a bowl.
Pour the cider vinegar, water, sugar, and salt into a saucepan and bring to a boil. Pour the hot liquid over the turnip cubes. Let cool at room temperature. Set aside in the refrigerator.

FOR THE FILLING

In a bowl, stir together all the ingredients to make a rich and creamy filling.

FOR THE YUZU GEL

Place all the ingredients in a saucepan and bring to a boil. Boil for 2 minutes, stirring constantly. Pour the mixture onto a high-sided baking sheet and place in the refrigerator.
When the gel has set, blend until smooth. Store it in a pipette in the refrigerator.

TO SERVE

Fill each tartlet with the filling. Arrange seven pickled turnip cubes on top of each tartlet. Using a spatula, spread the mixture so that the surface is smooth and even. Drain the turnip petals and arrange over the whole of the top of each tartlet. Garnish with a few dots of yuzu gel and some snipped chives.

ROOTS —— SPRING P. 30

KOHLRABI AND SHELLFISH

SERVES 4

FOR THE KOHLRABI

4 kohlrabi, each 4 in. (10 cm) in diameter

FOR THE SHELLFISH JUS

1 shallot, finely chopped
1/4 cup (55 ml) olive oil
2 1/4 lb. (1 kg) cockles
1/3 cup + 1 1/2 tbsp. (100 ml) water

FOR THE SHELLFISH

3 1/2 oz. (100 g) clams
3 1/2 oz. (100 g) cockles
3 1/2 oz. (100 g) brown Venus (smooth) clams
3 1/2 oz. (100 g) razor clams
3 1/2 oz. (100 g) bouchot (rope-grown) mussels
Shellfish jus

FOR THE SHELLFISH STOCK

3/4 oz. (20 g) fresh ginger
1/2 hot chile pepper
1/2 celery stalk
1/2 garlic clove
1/3 cup (1/2 oz./15 g) cilantro (fresh coriander)
7/8 cup (200 ml) shellfish jus
3 1/2 tbsp. (50 ml) lime juice
Unrefined sea salt

FOR THE HERB OIL

1 3/4 oz. (50 g) curly parsley
1 oz. (25 g) chives
1/2 oz. (15 g) cilantro (fresh coriander)
5 g dill
5 g tarragon
1 1/3 cups (320 ml) grapeseed oil

FOR THE GARNISH

1 lime
1 celery stalk
1 green apple

TO SERVE

12 cilantro (coriander) flowers
Crushed ice

FOR THE KOHLRABI

Clean the kohlrabi and cut off the tops (to serve as a lid). Using a melon baller, remove balls of kohlrabi from the insides until hollowed out. Work the inside and the lid to ensure a smooth finish. Set the emptied kohlrabi aside in the refrigerator. Place the kohlrabi balls in a bowl of iced water and set aside.

FOR THE SHELLFISH JUS

In a saucepan, sweat the shallot in the olive oil. Add the cockles and stir until they are hot. Add the water, cover, and let cook for about 15 minutes. Once cooked, all the shells should be open. Remove from the heat and strain through a chinois, reserving the jus. Let cool.

FOR THE SHELLFISH

Place all the shellfish in boiling water until opened. (Discard any shells that remain closed.) Cool in iced water. Clean the shellfish and set aside in the refrigerator in a little shellfish jus.

FOR THE SHELLFISH STOCK

Peel the ginger, seed the chile pepper, and finely dice them both as well as the celery, garlic, and cilantro (coriander). Blend all the ingredients. Strain through a chinois and refrigerate.

FOR THE HERB OIL

Blanch the herbs in boiling water for 1 minute, then cool in iced water. Squeeze to remove excess water. In a Thermomix®, blend the sunflower oil and the blanched herbs for 10 minutes at 158°F (70°C). Pour the oil into a container and let infuse overnight in the refrigerator.
The following day, strain the oil through a Superbag® without squeezing it. Reserve the strained oil and store it in a pipette in the refrigerator.

FOR THE GARNISH

Supreme the lime and dice the flesh. Cut the celery diagonally into thin strips. Set aside in iced water.
Peel the apple and make into balls using a 1/3 in. (8 mm) diameter melon baller. Set aside each ingredient in iced water.

TO SERVE

Place some kohlrabi and apple balls into each hollowed-out kohlrabi. Then place the various shellfish inside, adding volume. Add the drained lime cubes and celery strips. To serve, pour the shellfish stock into the kohlrabi to halfway up the shellfish. Finish with a few drops of herb oil and the cilantro (coriander) flowers.
Cover each kohlrabi with its lid. Place each whole kohlrabi onto a plate with some crushed ice.

ROOTS —— SPRING P. 32

CARROT, KUMQUAT, AND PORK BELLY TERRINE

SERVES 4

FOR THE PORK BELLY

3 1/4 lb. (1.5 kg) pork belly
1 leek, sliced
1 small piece of fresh ginger, peeled and sliced
1 star anise
Scant 1/4 cup (1 3/4 oz./50 g) muscovado sugar
2 tbsp. mirin
2 tbsp. soy sauce
4 tsp. black balsamic vinegar
8 cups (2 L) pork stock

FOR THE CARROT AND KUMQUAT TERRINE

1/3 cup + 1 1/2 tbsp. (100 ml) carrot juice (made in a juicer)
1/3 cup + 1 1/2 tbsp. (100 ml) mandarin juice
1 tsp. (2 g) agar-agar powder
3 1/2 oz. (100 g) kumquats
2 1/4 lb. (1 kg) carrots
Unrefined sea salt

FOR THE KUMQUAT PICKLES

1 3/4 oz. (50 g) kumquats
1/3 cup + 1 1/2 tbsp. (100 ml) black balsamic vinegar
1 3/4 tsp. (5 g) black peppercorns
1 thyme sprig

FOR THE PORK BELLY

Preheat the oven to 280°F (140°C/gas 1). Remove the rind from the pork belly. Sear it in a very hot skillet (frying pan). Set aside.

In the same pan, sauté the leek and ginger. Deglaze with a little water.

Place the pork belly, leek, and ginger into a deep baking pan.

In a bowl, mix together the star anise, sugar, mirin, soy sauce, and vinegar and pour over the pork. Pour over the water or stock. Cover the baking pan with foil and cook in the oven for 1 hour 30 minutes.

Once the meat is cooked, removed the bone. Let the pork cool in its cooking juices, then cut into slices. Reduce the stock until it is of sauce consistency.

FOR THE CARROT AND KUMQUAT TERRINE

In a saucepan, stir together the carrot and mandarin juices. Add the agar-agar and boil for 2 minutes while whisking. Keep it warm.

Clean the kumquats and cut them into slices, removing the pips. Peel the carrots and, using a mandoline, cut them into very thin (1.5 mm) slices. Place the carrots into an ovenproof dish, season with the salt, and cook in a steam oven at 210°F (100°C) for 2 minutes.

Layer the cooked carrots in a rectangular ceramic baking dish, brushing each layer with the carrot and mandarin juice. Add three layers of carrots, then one of kumquats, repeating this process to the top of the dish.

Cook the terrine in the oven at 280°F (140°C/gas 1) for 20–30 minutes. Remove from the oven and press down with a weight. Let cool in the refrigerator.

FOR THE KUMQUAT PICKLES

Clean the kumquats and cut them into slices, removing the pips. In a saucepan, heat the vinegar with the peppercorns and thyme. Immerse the kumquats in the liquid then remove from the heat and let cool.

ROOTS —— SPRING P. 34

FOR THE CARROT AND MANDARIN SAUCE

2 1/4 lb. (1 kg) carrots
2 1/4 lb. (1 kg) mandarins
1 tbsp. (10 g) cornstarch (cornflour)
1 tsp. (5 g) yellow miso
2/3 cup (5 oz./150 g) cold butter
Unrefined sea salt

FOR THE CARROT AND MANDARIN SAUCE

In a juicer, extract the juice from the carrots and mandarin oranges, keeping the two separate. Reduce them separately in a Rotavapor® (rotary evaporator) to obtain a concentrated juice, then mix 1/3 cup + 1 1/2 tbsp. (100 ml) of the concentrated carrot juice with 5/8 cup (150 ml) of the concentrated mandarin juice.
Pour into a saucepan, then thicken with the cornstarch (cornflour). Stir in the miso then whisk in the cold butter. Season with salt, then strain through a chinois.

TO SERVE

Cut the terrine into rectangles about 3 x 1 1/2 in. (8 x 4 cm) and 3/8 in. (1 cm) deep. In a hot skillet (frying pan), brown them on each side, without adding any fat, to give them a slightly burnt appearance. Brush with the carrot and mandarin sauce and heat in the salamander.
Cut the pork belly into rectangles the same size as the terrine. Glaze with the reduced cooking juices.
Place a piece of pork belly onto each plate and lay the carrot and kumquat terrine on top. Arrange a few kumquat pickles on the top and finish with the carrot and mandarin sauce on the side.

WASABI
AND GREEN APPLE

SERVES 4

FOR THE WASABI ICE CREAM

Scant 2 cups (450 ml) whole milk
1/2 cup + 1 1/2 tbsp. (140 ml) cream
1 tbsp. (3/4 oz./21 g) inverted sugar syrup
3 1/2 tbsp. (1 1/2 oz./40 g) superfine (caster) sugar
1/4 cup + 2 tsp. (1 1/4 oz./34 g) low-fat (semi-skimmed) powdered milk
3/4 cup (4 oz./115 g) dextrose
1/2 fresh wasabi root, peeled and grated

FOR THE PISTACHIO PRALINE

1/2 cup (3 1/2 oz./100 g) sugar
2 cups (8 3/4 oz./250 g) toasted pistachios
1/4 tsp. fleur de sel

FOR THE YOGURT FOAM

1 1/2 cups (375 ml) plain (natural) yogurt
1/2 cup (125 ml) cream
1/4 cup + 1 tbsp. (1 1/4 oz./35 g) confectioners' (icing) sugar

FOR THE GREEN APPLE GRANITA

1 lb. 2 oz. (500 g) Granny Smith apples
2 tbsp. (1 oz./25 g) superfine (caster) sugar
5 tsp. water
1/4 tsp. ascorbic acid

FOR THE WASABI ICE CREAM

In a saucepan, heat the milk, cream, and inverted sugar syrup to 104°F (40°C). Add the sugar, powdered milk, and dextrose. Bring the mixture up to 185°F (85°C), then chill to 39°F (4°C). Blend the cold ice cream base with the wasabi. Let stand overnight in the refrigerator.
Strain through a chinois, then churn in an ice cream maker.

FOR THE PISTACHIO PRALINE

Make a dry caramel with the sugar: heat the sugar in a skillet (frying pan) until dark caramel in color. Remove from the heat and pour the syrup onto a silicone baking mat. Let cool, then weigh out 2 3/4 oz. (75 g) for the praline.
In a Thermomix®, blend the pistachios and the fleur de sel with the caramel until you have a creamy paste. Transfer to a pastry (piping) bag.

FOR THE YOGURT FOAM

In a bowl, using a whisk, mix together all the ingredients, being sure to remove any lumps. Pour into a siphon fitted with a gas cartridge and chill.

FOR THE GREEN APPLE GRANITA

Wash the apples then cut them into pieces, removing the pips but not the peel. In a blender, mix the apples with the sugar, water, and ascorbic acid. Strain the mixture through a chinois, pressing down using a ladle. Pour the liquid into a small freezer-proof container and freeze. Once it is hard, scrape it with a fork. Set aside in the freezer.

TO SERVE

Place a teaspoon of the pistachio praline into a glass bowl then add a scoop of wasabi ice cream in the center. Siphon the yogurt foam around it. Cover everything with the green apple granita.

ROOTS —— SPRING P. 36

MENTON ONION,
CARAMOTE SHRIMP, AND RED SHISO

SERVES 4

FOR THE RED SHISO TEA
1 1/4 cups (300 ml) water
1 oz. (30 g) red shiso leaves
2 1/2 tsp. (1/3 oz./10 g) citric acid

FOR THE ONION PICKLES
1 Menton onion
1 1/4 cups (300 ml) red shiso tea
5/8 cup (150 ml) cider vinegar
1/2 cup (3 1/2 oz./100 g) superfine (caster) sugar
1 tsp. (5 g) juniper berries
1/3 oz. (10 g) red shiso leaves

FOR THE CARAMOTE SHRIMP (PRAWN) TARTARE
8 San Remo caramote shrimp (prawns)
1 tsp. (5 g) finely chopped shallot
2 fresh lemon balm leaves, finely shredded
Zest and juice of 1 untreated lime
1 tsp. colatura di alici (Italian fermented anchovy sauce)
Unrefined sea salt

FOR THE SHELLFISH CONSOMMÉ
Shrimp (prawn) shells and heads
2 cups + 1 tbsp. (500 ml) water
1 lemongrass stalk
1/3 oz. (10 g) fresh ginger, peeled

FOR THE LIME GEL
1 cup (250 ml) lime juice
3 1/2 tsp. (1/4 oz./7 g) agar-agar powder

FOR THE RED SHISO TEA

In a saucepan, heat the water to 176°F (80°C). Add the shiso leaves and the citric acid. Let infuse for 10 minutes. Once the water has turned red, strain. Reserve the water.

FOR THE ONION PICKLES

Peel the onion, then cut it in half vertically. Separate the layers.
In a saucepan, mix the shisho tea with the vinegar, sugar, juniper berries, and shiso leaves. Bring to a boil, then add the onion. Let cool.

FOR THE CARAMOTE SHRIMP (PRAWN) TARTARE

Clean the shrimp (prawns), removing their shells and heads. Reserve these for the consommé. Dice the flesh, place in a bowl, and season with the shallot, lemon balm, lime zest and juice, and the colatura di alici. Adjust the seasoning with unrefined sea salt. Set aside in the refrigerator.

FOR THE SHELLFISH CONSOMMÉ

In a stand mixer fitted with the paddle attachment, crush the shrimp shells and heads to a smooth paste.
Put this paste into a saucepan and fill with the cold water, then slowly bring to a boil. The proteins in the shrimp will bind and solidify on the surface of the stock. Using a ladle, transfer to a chinois lined with paper to strain it. The stock should be clear. Pour into a clean saucepan and add the lemongrass and ginger. Reduce over low heat, then season with unrefined sea salt. Strain and let cool.

FOR THE LIME GEL

In a saucepan, boil the lime juice with the agar-agar for 2 minutes, while whisking continuously with a whisk. Let cool, then blend. Transfer to a pipette and set aside.

(RECIPE CONTINUES OVERLEAF)

FOR THE HERB OIL
1 3/4 oz. (50 g) parsley
1 oz. (25 g) chives
1/2 oz. (15 g) cilantro (fresh coriander)
5 g dill
5 g tarragon
1 1/4 cups (300 ml) sunflower oil

FOR THE LEMONGRASS OIL
1 3/4 oz. (50 g) lemongrass stalk (about 2 stalks)
7/8 cup (200 ml) sunflower oil

FOR THE GARNISH
4 1/4 cups (1 L) water
1/4 cup (1 3/4 oz./50 g) tapioca
1 lime

FOR THE HERB OIL

Blanch the herbs in boiling water for 1 minute, then cool in iced water. Squeeze them to remove excess water. In a Thermomix®, blend the sunflower oil and the blanched herbs for 10 minutes at 158°F (70°C). Pour the oil into a container and let infuse overnight in the refrigerator.

The following day, strain the oil through a Superbag® without squeezing it. Reserve the strained oil and store it in a pipette in the refrigerator.

FOR THE LEMONGRASS OIL

Finely chop the lemongrass and place in a Thermomix® with the oil. Blend at 158°F (70°C) for 10 minutes. Strain through a Superbag® without squeezing it. Transfer the strained oil to a pipette and set aside in the refrigerator.

FOR THE GARNISH

In a saucepan, boil the water with a little salt. Add the tapioca and cook for 5 minutes, then rinse under cold water and drain. Let the tapioca swell in a little of the shellfish consommé. Set aside in the refrigerator.

Remove all the peel and pith from the lime then dice. Set aside.

TO SERVE

Drain the pickled onion petals then fill each one with a spoonful of the shrimp tartare. Cut the stuffed onion lengthwise into five slices to make it easier to eat. Arrange them together to keep the onion shape.

In a bowl, mix the tapioca with the shellfish consommé.

Place stuffed onion pickles in a dish. Arrange a few dots of lime gel and the diced lime around the edge. Pour in the tapioca consommé. Finish with a few drops of the herb oil and a few drops of the lemongrass oil.

NEW POTATO RAGOUT

SERVES 4

FOR THE POTATOES
7 oz. (200 g) new potatoes
1 thyme sprig
1 bay leaf
Scant 1/4 cup (1 3/4 oz./50 g) unsalted butter

FOR THE RAGOUT
1/3 oz. (10 g) cod tripe
Knob of butter
1 tsp. (5 g) finely chopped shallot
Elderflower vinegar
1 tbsp. (3 g) snipped chives
Unrefined sea salt

FOR THE YOUNG GARLIC FOAM
5 oz. (150 g) young garlic
3 1/2 oz. (100 g) new potatoes
1 1/4 cups (300 ml) cream
Unrefined sea salt

FOR THE POTATO TUILE
1 lb. 2 oz. (500 g) potatoes
4 tsp. (1/3 oz./10 g) xanthan gum
Sunflower oil

FOR THE POTATOES

Clean the potatoes in cold water. Place them in a Dutch oven (casserole dish) and cover with cold water. Add the thyme, bay leaf, and butter. Bring slowly to a boil. Once the potatoes are cooked, let them cool in the cooking water. Peel them using a small knife and set aside in the cooking water.

FOR THE RAGOUT

Cut the cod tripe into brunoises. In a large skillet (frying pan), heat the butter and sweat the shallot. Add the drained potatoes and the cod tripe. Season with a drizzle of vinegar and some salt. Finish with the chives.

FOR THE YOUNG GARLIC FOAM

Preheat the oven to 360°F (180°C/gas 4). Peel the garlic. Place the cloves in a saucepan of cold water, bring to a boil, then drain. Repeat this blanching process three times. Bake the potatoes in foil in the oven for 40 minutes. Once they are well cooked, remove the flesh from the skins and set aside.
In a saucepan, reduce the cream by half. In a Thermomix®, blend the potato flesh, reduced cream, blanched garlic, and some salt until smooth. Transfer to a small siphon fitted with two gas cartridges. Keep warm.

FOR THE POTATO TUILE

Cook the whole unpeeled potatoes in a saucepan of boiling water, then peel them and mix the flesh in a Thermomix® with the xanthan gum until smooth. Transfer to a pastry (piping) bag fitted with a plain tip (nozzle) and pipe the tuiles by drawing little roots on a silicone baking mat. (The mixture should be lukewarm.) Let harden. Fry the potato tuile in sunflower oil at 355°F (180°C). Drain on paper towels.

TO SERVE

Place some ragout in a dish. Cover with the garlic foam and top with the potato tuile.

ROOTS —— SUMMER P. 42

FISH, **LICORICE**, AND **BLACK GARLIC**

SERVES 4

FOR THE BLACK CRISPS
1/2 cup (3 1/2 oz/100 g) carnaroli rice
1 cup + 1 tbsp. (250 ml) water
4 tsp. squid ink
1/4 tsp. unrefined sea salt
4 1/4 cups (1 L) sunflower oil

FOR THE BLACK VEIL
3 1/2 oz. (100 g) black garlic
1/4 cup (60 ml) water
Scant 1/8 tsp. (0.2 g) xanthan gum
1 tbsp. squid ink

FOR THE FISH
1 scorpionfish (or other sustainable fish from your region) about 14 oz. (400 g)
4 tsp. (3/4 oz./20 g) clarified butter

FOR THE LICORICE HOLLANDAISE
4 egg yolks
5 tsp. water
5 tsp. lemon juice
1/2 cup (4 1/2 oz./125 g) clarified butter
1 tbsp. (1/2 oz./12 g) powdered licorice
3 tbsp. (1 oz./25 g) vegetable carbon
Unrefined sea salt

FOR THE BLACK CRISPS

Cook the rice in the water. It needs to be very well cooked. Strain through a chinois. In a Thermomix®, blend the cooked rice with the squid ink and salt. Spread the resulting paste out on a silicone baking mat in a very thin (3 mm) layer. Let dry in a desiccator for 4 hours.

Once the paste is dry, cut it into pieces and fry in sunflower oil at 425°F (220°C) until the crisps have puffed up. Place on paper towels in a container.

FOR THE BLACK VEIL

Peel the black garlic and blend. Add enough water to the blender to obtain a smooth paste, then add the xanthan gum and squid ink and blend well. Once the mixture is smooth, strain through a sieve.

Spread the black paste out on a silicone baking mat in a very thin (2 mm) layer. Let dry at room temperature. When it is dry, but still slightly supple, cut into rectangles of about 4 x 2 in. (10 x 5 cm) and store in a sealed container.

FOR THE FISH

Fillet the fish. Heat a skillet (frying pan) with a drizzle of olive oil, then add the fish fillets, skin side down, and cook over low heat for 8 minutes. Let rest for a few minutes before cutting into 3/4 in. (2 cm) slices.

Totally cover each fish portion with a black veil. Brush with clarified butter.

FOR THE LICORICE HOLLANDAISE

In a skillet (frying pan), combine the egg yolks, water, lemon juice and some unrefined sea salt. Heat gently while whisking vigorously to stir in air until creamy. Gradually add the melted or warm clarified butter, whisking constantly over low heat. Stir in the powdered licorice and the vegetable carbon. If necessary, season to taste with more lemon juice or licorice. It should be liquid. Pour into a small siphon fitted with two gas cartridges. Keep warm.

TO SERVE

On a plate, place the black-veiled fish on the left. Add a little licorice hollandaise beside it. Finally, cover the hollandaise with a black crisp.

ROOTS —— SUMMER P. 46

TURMERIC AND APRICOT

SERVES 4

FOR THE YOGURT FOAM
MAKES ABOUT 10 PORTIONS
5 tsp. water
2 tbsp. (1 oz./25 g) superfine (caster) sugar
3 silver gelatin leaves (8 g)
1 2/3 cups (400 ml) plain (natural) yogurt

FOR THE TURMERIC ICE CREAM
MAKES ABOUT 30 PORTIONS
2 1/4 tsp. (6 g) carob flour
1/4 cup (1 3/4 oz./50 g) superfine (caster) sugar
2 1/3 cups (550 ml) whole milk
1/2 cup (120 ml) cream
1/3 cup + 1/2 tbsp. (1 1/2 oz./42 g) powdered milk
3/4 cup + 2 tbsp. (4 3/4 oz./137 g) dextrose
3 1/2 tsp. (1 oz./26 g) inverted sugar syrup
2 1/4 oz. (60 g) fresh turmeric root, peeled

FOR THE PISTACHIO PRALINE
MAKES ABOUT 30 PORTIONS
1/4 cup (1 3/4 oz./50 g) superfine (caster) sugar
4 tsp. water
2 cups (8 3/4 oz./250 g) pistachios, toasted
1 tbsp. pistachio oil

FOR THE APRICOT VEIL
4 apricots

TO SERVE
12 toasted pistachios
Voatsiperifery (Madagascar wild) pepper

FOR THE YOGURT FOAM

Make a syrup with the water and sugar. Soak the gelatin leaves in a little cold water. Squeeze dry, then dissolve in the warm syrup. Stir this syrup into the yogurt. Pour into a small siphon fitted with a gas cartridge. Set aside in the refrigerator.

FOR THE TURMERIC ICE CREAM

In a bowl, mix the carob flour with the sugar.
In a saucepan, heat the milk and cream. Add the powdered milk, dextrose, and inverted sugar syrup. When it reaches 104°F (40°C), add the carob flour and sugar mixture. Heat to 185°F (85°C).
Blend the turmeric root with the warm ice cream base. Strain through a Superbag®, chill to 39°F (4°C), then let rest for 12 hours at this temperature.
Churn in an ice cream maker. Set aside in the freezer.

FOR THE PISTACHIO PRALINE

In a saucepan, heat the sugar and water to 250°F (121°C) without stirring. Remove from the heat and stir in the pistachios. Once the sugar has crystallized, return the pistachios to the heat to caramelize them.
Pour the mixture onto a silicone baking mat, let cool, then mix in a Thermomix® with the pistachio oil to make praline.

FOR THE APRICOT VEIL

Wash the apricots then cut them in half and remove the pit (stone). Using a knife, slice the apricot halves thinly into half-moons.
Layer these apricot slices, from top to bottom, on a sheet of guitar paper. Then, using a cookie (pastry) cutter, cut out rounds the same diameter as your dessert dish.

TO SERVE

Spread a teaspoon of pistachio praline in a small bowl and add three toasted pistachios. Place a good spoonful of turmeric ice cream in the center. Fill the bowl with the yogurt foam and use a spatula to smooth the surface. Sprinkle with a little pepper, then cover with the apricot veil.

ROOTS —— SUMMER P. 48

BEET AND CAVIAR

SERVES 4

FOR THE BEET (BEETROOT)
4 1/2 lb. (2 kg) Guérande unrefined sea salt
7/8 cup (200 ml) water
1 crapaudine beet (beetroot)

FOR THE CAVIAR SAUCE
1 1/2 tbsp. (28 g) Ossetra caviar
1/4 cup (60 ml) whipping cream

FOR THE BEET (BEETROOT)

Preheat a dry oven to 350°F (180°C/gas 4). Place the salt in a bowl and stir in the water. Line an ovenproof dish with parchment (baking) paper, then spread with a fine layer of the salt. Place the beet (beetroot) on top and cover completely with the remainder of the salt.
Cook the beet in the oven for about 3 hours. Check for doneness using a cooking probe. Remove from the oven and let rest for 30 minutes at room temperature. Remove from its salt crust and peel.
Using a meat slicer, cut the beet into very thin (1/8 in./3 mm) slices.

FOR THE CAVIAR SAUCE

In a bowl, stir the caviar into the cream.

TO SERVE

In a dish, arrange the warm beet strips in a pile. Pour the caviar sauce over the top.

CELERY ROOT
AND SQUID TAGLIATELLE

SERVES 4

FOR THE SQUID TAGLIATELLE
1 large whole squid

FOR THE CELERY ROOT (CELERIAC) MOUSSE
1 large celery root (celeriac)
1/3 cup + 2 tbsp. (3 1/2 oz./100 g) butter
Milk
Unrefined sea salt

FOR THE CITRUS PURÉE
7 oz. (200 g) preserved lemon
3 1/2 oz. (100 g) preserved citron
Lemon juice

FOR THE CELERY ROOT (CELERIAC) TAGLIATELLE
1 celery root (celeriac)
Scant 1/4 cup (1 3/4 oz./50 g) butter
1 thyme sprig
Lemon juice
Unrefined sea salt

FOR THE CELERY ROOT (CELERIAC) AND GRAPEFRUIT TARTARE
The reserved celery root (celeriac) peel
1 pink grapefruit
5 lemon balm leaves, finely shredded
Olive oil
Unrefined sea salt

FOR THE VERMOUTH SAUCE
Scant 1/4 cup (1 oz./30 g) finely chopped shallot
3/4 cup + 2 tbsp. (7 oz./200 g) butter
1/3 cup (80 ml) dry white vermouth
2 tbsp. white wine
7/8 cup (200 ml) shellfish jus
Unrefined sea salt

FOR THE SQUID TAGLIATELLE

Open the squid in the middle and remove and discard the tentacles and entrails. Remove the double skin on the inside and outside. Cut the squid into rectangles, then place it in four layers and freeze.
Using a mandoline, cut into very thin 1/8 in. (3 mm) strips. Set aside in the refrigerator.

FOR THE CELERY ROOT (CELERIAC) MOUSSE

Peel and finely chop the celery root (celeriac). In a large saucepan, sweat the celery root in the butter without browning. Cover and let cook over low heat. If necessary, add a little milk. Season with unrefined sea salt. Once the celery root is well cooked, blend it to a very smooth purée.

FOR THE CITRUS PURÉE

Chop the preserved lemon and citron, then blend to a very smooth purée. If needed, add a little lemon juice to obtain the desired consistency. Strain through a sieve and set aside in the refrigerator.

FOR THE CELERY ROOT (CELERIAC) TAGLIATELLE

Peel the celery root, keeping its round shape. Reserve the peel for the celery root and grapefruit tartare. Slice the celery root into strips using a Japanese turning slicer. Using a knife, cut these strips into ribbons the same size as the squid tagliatelle.
In a saucepan, melt the butter with the thyme sprig. Cook the celery root tagliatelle in this glaze, then season with lemon juice and salt.

FOR THE CELERY ROOT (CELERIAC) AND GRAPEFRUIT TARTARE

Cut the celery root peel into brunoise. Supreme the grapefruit and dice the flesh. In a bowl, stir together the celery root, grapefruit, and shredded lemon balm. Season with olive oil and unrefined sea salt. Set aside.

FOR THE VERMOUTH SAUCE

In a saucepan, sweat the shallot with a knob of butter. Add the vermouth, wine, and shellfish jus. Cook for about 15 minutes. Strain into a skillet (frying pan). Heat, and gradually add the remaining butter, whisking continuously until you have a creamy sauce. Season with unrefined sea salt. Keep warm.

TO SERVE

Place a quenelle of the celery root mousse in the center of a dish. Add a small quenelle of the citrus purée to one side. Add a tablespoon of the celery root and grapefruit tartare.
In a skillet (frying pan), heat the celery root and squid tagliatelle. Using a ladle and tongs, roll up the tagliatelle. Place on top of the celery root mousse. Finally, coat with the vermouth sauce.

ROOTS —— FALL P. 54

ASSORTED **POTATO** GNOCCHI

SERVES 4

FOR THE POTATO GNOCCHI
7 oz. (200 g) potato (1 medium potato)
1 cup (4 1/2 oz./130 g) all-purpose (plain) flour
1/4 cup + 1 tbsp. (2 1/2 oz./70 g) fresh ricotta
2 1/2 tbsp. (1/2 oz./16 g) grated Parmesan
1 tsp. (6 g) beurre noisette
1/3 oz. (10 g) egg yolk
1/4 tsp. unrefined sea salt
Pinch ground black pepper

FOR THE POTATO AND BEET (BEETROOT) GNOCCHI
7 oz. (200 g) potato (1 medium potato)
1 cup (4 1/2 oz./130 g) all-purpose (plain) flour
1/4 cup + 1 tbsp. (2 1/2 oz./70 g) fresh ricotta
2 1/2 tbsp. (1/2 oz./16 g) grated Parmesan
1 tsp. (6 g) beurre noisette
1/3 oz. (10 g) egg yolk
2 tbsp. beet (beetroot) juice
1/4 tsp. unrefined sea salt
Pinch ground black pepper

FOR THE SWEET POTATO GNOCCHI
7 oz. (200 g) sweet potato (1 medium)
1 cup (4 1/2 oz./130 g) all-purpose (plain) flour
1/4 cup + 1 tbsp. (2 1/2 oz./70 g) fresh ricotta
2 1/2 tbsp. (1/2 oz./16 g) grated Parmesan
1 tsp. (6 g) beurre noisette
1/3 oz. (10 g) egg yolk
1/4 tsp. unrefined sea salt
Pinch ground black pepper

FOR THE 'VITELOTTE' POTATO GNOCCHI
7 oz. (200 g) potato (1 medium potato)
3/4 cup (3 1/2 oz./100 g) all-purpose (plain) flour ('Vitelotte' potatoes are much drier than normal ones, so require less flour.)
1/4 cup + 1 tbsp. (2 1/2 oz./70 g) fresh ricotta
2 1/2 tbsp. (1/2 oz./16 g) grated Parmesan
1 tsp. (6 g) beurre noisette
1/3 oz. (10 g) egg yolk
1/4 tsp. unrefined sea salt
Pinch ground black pepper

TO COOK THE GNOCCHI
8 cups (2 L) water
2 tsp. unrefined sea salt
1 stick less 1 tbsp. (3 1/2 oz./100 g) cold butter, diced

FOR ALL THE GNOCCHI

Preheat the oven to 355°F (180°C/gas 4). Wash the potatoes and sweet potato and bake them "en papillote" in the oven for 40 minutes. They should be very soft. Peel them, then pass them, separately, through a food mill. Put each potato into a separate bowl and add all the remaining ingredients. Mix by hand, without overworking the dough.

Form into pieces of about 1 3/4 oz. (50 g). Dust the work surface with flour, then roll out each dough into a very thin sausage shape. Using a knife, cut into gnocchi. Set aside on a baking sheet dusted with flour.

COOKING THE GNOCCHI

In a large saucepan, boil the water with a little salt. Add the gnocchi and cook for 3 minutes. Drain, then tip them in a skillet (frying pan).

Add the cold diced butter and stir with the gnocchi for 5 minutes over low heat until the butter has melted. They should be creamy.

ROOTS —— FALL P. 56

FOR THE GOAT CHEESE SAUCE

1/3 cup + 1 1/2 tbsp. (100 ml) whipping cream
3/4 cup + 2 tbsp. (3 1/2 oz./100 g) fresh goat cheese
1/2 tsp. unrefined sea salt

FOR THE CELERY ROOT (CELERIAC) AND COFFEE SAUCE

1 celery root (celeriac)
4 tsp. (20 ml) olive oil
4 1/4 cups (1 L) water
1/2 tbsp. (3 g) coffee beans
2 sage leaves
1 tsp. (5 g) soy sauce
1 stick less 1 tbsp. (3 1/2 oz./100 g) cold butter, diced

TO SERVE

1/2 preserved lemon
2 coffee beans

FOR THE GOAT CHEESE SAUCE

Place all the ingredients into a Thermomix®, then mix on speed 2 for 20 minutes at 140°F (60°C). Keep warm.

FOR THE CELERY ROOT (CELERIAC) AND COFFEE SAUCE

Preheat the oven to 350°F (180°C/gas 4). Wash the celery root (celeriac) well. Dice the flesh and place in a stainless-steel container with the peel and a drizzle of olive oil. Cook in the oven for 30 minutes. Once the celery root is golden, transfer to a saucepan and add the water, coffee beans, sage leaves, and soy sauce. Simmer gently until reduced by a quarter (about 1 hour).
Strain through a chinois and reserve the liquid. Add the cold diced butter and whisk until the sauce is smooth.

TO SERVE

Remove the peel from the preserved lemon and cut into 1/4 in (5 mm) cubes. Place three cubes of preserved lemon in a dish. Cover with the gnocchi. Add a tablespoon of each sauce. Grate a little coffee over the top.

GINGER AND PENJA WHITE PEPPER

SERVES 4

FOR THE GINGER ICE CREAM
3 1/2 oz. (100 g) fresh ginger
1 3/4 cups (420 ml) milk
1/2 cup + 1 tbsp. (129 ml) whipping cream
1 tbsp. (3/4 oz./20 g) inverted sugar syrup
2/3 cup (3 3/4 oz./102 g) dextrose
1/4 cup (1 oz./30 g) powdered milk
3 tbsp. (1 1/4 oz./35 g) superfine (caster) sugar
Scant 1/2 tsp. (1 g) carob flour

FOR THE GINGER CUSTARD
1 1/2 silver gelatin leaves (3.75 g)
1/2 cup (125 ml) milk
1/2 cup (125 ml) whipping cream
3 tbsp. (1 1/4 oz./35 g) superfine (caster) sugar
1 tsp. (5 g) green cardamom seeds, crushed
1 cup (8 3/4 oz./250 g) Matsoni yogurt
2/3 tsp. (2.5 g) grated, peeled fresh ginger

FOR THE CANDIED GINGER
1 1/4 cups (8 3/4 oz./250 g) superfine (caster) sugar
4 1/4 cups (1 L) water
4 1/2 oz. (125 g) fresh ginger

FOR THE GINGER AND LEMONGRASS MARMALADE
1/3 cup + 1 1/2 tbsp. (100 ml) lemon juice
1/3 cup + 1 1/2 tbsp. (100 ml) ginger juice (from 7 oz./200 g fresh ginger)
1/3 cup + 1 1/2 tbsp. (100 ml) water
3 1/2 tbsp. (1 1/2 oz./40 g) superfine (caster) sugar
2 1/2 tsp. (5 g) agar-agar powder
2/3 tsp. citric acid
1 lemongrass stalk
1 lemon
Candied ginger (see above)

FOR THE LEMON AND GINGER MERINGUE
2/3 cup (4 3/4 oz./135 g) superfine (caster) sugar
3 1/2 oz. (100 g) egg whites
1 1/2 tbsp. (1/4 oz./8 g) powdered egg white
1/3 cup (75 ml) lemon juice
4 tsp. (20 ml) ginger juice
1 oz. (30 g) Nougasec (Louis François®)

FOR THE GINGER ICE CREAM

Peel the ginger and, in a juicer, juice to obtain 1/3 cup (75 ml) of ginger juice. In a saucepan, heat the milk, cream, inverted sugar syrup, dextrose, powdered milk, and sugar to 104°F (40°C). Stir in the carob flour and heat to 185°F (85°C). Remove from the heat and let cool to 39°F (4°C) in the refrigerator. Let mature 25 hours, then stir in the ginger juice. Blend using an immersion blender, then churn in an ice cream maker. Store in the freezer at 5°F (-15°C).

FOR THE GINGER CUSTARD

Soak the gelatin in a little water. In a saucepan, heat the milk, cream, and sugar to 140°F (60°C), then add the crushed cardamom seeds. Let infuse for 20 minutes. Stir in the yogurt and the grated fresh ginger. Heat the mixture, then remove from the heat and stir in the drained gelatin. Strain through a chinois, then pour the mixture into a 12 in. (30 cm) square stainless-steel container. It should be about 1/2 in. (1 cm) thick. Let cool in the refrigerator for 3 hours. Once the custard has set, cut out four circles using a 3 1/4 in. (8 cm) diameter cookie (pastry) cutter.

FOR THE CANDIED GINGER

In a saucepan, make a syrup with the sugar and half the water (2 cups + 2 tbsp./ 500 ml). Set aside.

Peel and finely chop the ginger. In a saucepan, blanch the ginger three times in the remaining (2 cups + 2 tbsp./500 ml) water, then transfer the ginger to the syrup. Cook over a low heat for 1 hour under a parchment (baking) paper lid. Once the ginger is soft, remove from the heat and conserve at room temperature.

FOR THE GINGER AND LEMONGRASS MARMALADE

In a saucepan, bring to a boil the lemon juice, ginger juice, water, sugar, agar-agar, citric acid, and lemongrass, then simmer over low heat for about 2 hours. Remove the lemongrass, then let cool to room temperature. Store in the refrigerator until cold, then blend.

Using a knife, supreme the lemon and dice the flesh. Add the candied ginger and the diced lemon to the marmalade mixture.

FOR THE LEMON AND GINGER MERINGUE

Preheat the oven to 200°F (90°C). Mix all the ingredients together in a mixer. Spread circles out onto a silicone baking mat using a 3 1/4 in. (8 cm) diameter round template. Bake in the oven for 1 hour.

ROOTS —— FALL P. 58

FOR THE GINGER OPALINE
10 1/2 oz. (300 g) fondant
1/3 cup + 1 tbsp. (7 oz./200 g) glucose syrup
2 3/4 oz. (75 g) Nougasec (Louis François®)
1 tsp. (2 g) ground ginger
Gold powder
Silver powder

FOR THE PENJA WHITE PEPPER FOAM
2 tbsp. (1 oz./25 g) superfine (caster) sugar
5 tsp. (25 ml) water
2 cups + 2 tbsp. (500 ml) whole milk
3/4 oz. (20 g) Penja white pepper
(1/3 tsp. ground)
1 oz. (25 g) Pro Espuma (Sosa®, stabilizer)

FOR THE GINGER OPALINE

In a saucepan, mix the fondant, glucose, and Nougasec and cook at 290°F (145°C). Pour the mixture onto a silicone baking mat and let cool. Once hard, mix to a fine powder in a Thermomix®. Using a 3 1/4 in. (8 cm) diameter round template, sprinkle the powder onto a silicone baking mat, then sprinkle with the ground ginger. Using a pastry (piping) bag, pipe little circles on top to create little "craters" as on the moon. Melt in the oven at 340°F (170°C/gas 4) for 3 minutes. Let cool, then brush with the gold and silver powders.

FOR THE PENJA WHITE PEPPER FOAM

In a saucepan, dissolve the sugar in the water. Set aside.
In a Thermomix®, mix the cold milk with the pepper. Pour into a stainless-steel container, then let infuse in the refrigerator for 6 hours. Strain then stir in the sugar syrup and the Pro Espuma. Bring to a boil, then cool in the refrigerator. Once the mixture is cold, blend using an immersion blender then pour into a siphon fitted with two gas cartridges.

TO SERVE

Place a teaspoon of the ginger and lemongrass marmalade in the center of a dish. Cover with a disk of ginger custard. Add a quenelle of the ginger ice cream, then cover everything with the Penja white pepper foam. Add a meringue and top with the opaline.

ROOTS —— FALL P. 58

ONION AND COMTÉ CUBE

SERVES 4

FOR THE PANKO CUBES

1 cup + 2 tbsp. (7 oz./200 g) clarified butter
2 eggs
1/3 cup + 1 tbsp. (1 3/4 oz./50 g) all-purpose (plain) flour
1 1/4 cups (3 1/2 oz./100 g) panko
Unrefined sea salt
Sunflower oil

FOR THE COMTÉ FOAM

2 cups + 2 tbsp. (50 ml) cream
1 ¾ cups (7 oz./200 g) shredded (grated) Comté cheese 36 months
2 egg whites

FOR THE FRIED ONION

2 white onions
Sunflower oil

TO SERVE

1/3 oz. (10 g) Comté cheese
Fleur de sel
Thyme flowers
Thyme shoots

FOR THE PANKO CUBES

Melt the clarified butter, then pour into a square silicone candy mold with 3/4 in. (2 cm) square cavities. Freeze.

In a bowl, beat the eggs and season with a little salt. Spread out the flour, beaten egg, and panko on three separate plates. Stick a toothpick into each frozen clarified butter cube. Dip them in the flour, then in the beaten egg, and finally in the panko. Repeat this process three more times with the egg and panko. Press the edges well to maintain a square shape. Freeze.

Once the cubes are hard, remove the toothpicks and slice ¼ in. (5 mm) off the top of the cubes. Return them to the freezer.

Heat the sunflower oil to 355°F (180°C). Fry the cubes for a few minutes. The butter should melt and the panko coating should be golden. Remove any excess oil and dry well on paper towels. Place the cubes in a desiccator to keep them crispy.

FOR THE COMTÉ FOAM

In a saucepan, reduce the cream by half. Pour into a Thermomix® and mix gently with the shredded (grated) Comté. Once the cheese has melted, add the egg whites and mix for a few seconds until smooth.

Pour the mixture into a siphon fitted with two gas cartridges. Set aside at room temperature.

FOR THE FRIED ONION

Peel and grate the onions and drain well. Fry the onions in the sunflower oil at 320°F (160°C) for about 8 minutes until golden brown. Drain on paper towels.

TO SERVE

Using a mandoline, thinly slice the Comté, then cut into squares using a 3/8 in. (1 cm) square cookie (pastry) cutter. Place a slice of Comté into each panko cube. Fill with the Comté foam. Top with the fried onion. Garnish with a few grains of fleur de sel and the thyme flowers and shoots.

ROOTS —— WINTER P. 60

ASSORTED **RADISH**, FISH, AND CITRUS FRUIT ROSETTE

SERVES 4

FOR THE KAFFIR LIME LEAF OIL
1 3/4 oz. (50 g) kaffir lime leaves
Scant 1 cup (225 ml) grapeseed oil

FOR THE FISH
1 leerfish or amberjack fillet
(or other sustainable fish
from your region), skin removed
5/8 cup (150 ml) kaffir lime leaf oil
2 tbsp. (30 g) salt

FOR THE ORANGE GELATIN
1 silver gelatin leaf (3 g)
3/4 cup + 1 tbsp. (190 ml) orange juice
1 1/2 tsp. (3 g) agar-agar powder

FOR THE GRAPEFRUIT GELATIN
1 silver gelatin leaf (3 g)
3/4 cup + 1 tbsp. (190 ml) grapefruit juice
1 1/2 tsp. (3 g) agar-agar powder
4 tsp. (16 g) superfine (caster) sugar

FOR THE PLANKTON GELATIN
2 silver gelatin leaves (5 g)
1 5/8 cups (385 ml) water
1/4 tsp. (0.5 g) plankton
2 1/2 tsp. (5 g) agar-agar powder
Zest of 2 untreated limes

FOR THE CITRUS BOUILLON
1/2 oz. (15 g) kombu (dried kelp)
2 cups + 1 tbsp. (500 ml) water
1 oz. (25 g) katsuobushi (bonito flakes)
1 tsp. yuzu juice
Zest of 1 untreated lime
Zest of 1 untreated orange
Zest of 1 untreated lemon
Zest of 1 untreated grapefruit
2 tsp. soy sauce
Unrefined sea salt

FOR THE YUZU JELLY
1/2 cup (125 ml) yuzu juice
1 cup + 1 tbsp. (250 ml) water
2 1/2 tbsp. superfine (caster) sugar
4 tsp. (1/4 oz./8 g) agar-agar powder

FOR THE RADISHES
1 'Green Meat' radish
1 'Red Meat' radish
1 daikon

TO SERVE
Fleur de sel

FOR THE KAFFIR LIME LEAF OIL

Blend the kaffir lime leaves and the oil in a Thermomix® at speed 10 for 30 seconds. Let infuse in the refrigerator overnight.
The following day, strain it through a Superbag® without squeezing it. Store it in a pipette in the refrigerator.

FOR THE FISH

Place the fish fillet, oil, and salt in a sous-vide bag. Cook at 108°F (42°C) in a sous-vide cooker or steam oven. Chill in a bowl of iced water. Cut the fish into sashimi-style strips.

FOR THE GELATINS

For each gelatin, proceed in the same way: soak the gelatin leaf in a little iced water. Place the remaining ingredients in a saucepan and bring to a boil. Boil for 2 minutes, stirring constantly with a whisk. Remove from the heat and stir in the drained gelatin. Transfer the mixture to a piston funnel, then spread it very thinly onto cold marble. Using a 2 in. (5 cm) diameter cookie (pastry) cutter, cut into disks, then cut each disk in half to make half-moons. Set aside in the refrigerator.

FOR THE CITRUS BOUILLON

Infuse the kombu in the water at 140°F (60°C) for 2 hours. Remove the kombu, bring the water to a boil, and add the katsuobushi (bonito flakes). Infuse for 1 minute then strain and let cool.
Mix the remaining ingredients together with the cold bouillon. Let infuse for 20 minutes. Strain and set aside in the refrigerator.

FOR THE YUZU JELLY

Place all the ingredients in a saucepan and bring to a boil. Boil for 2 minutes, stirring constantly. Let cool, blend, then transfer to a pipette.

FOR THE RADISHES

Cut the radishes into very thin (2 mm) slices. Blanch in boiling water for 30 seconds. Cool in iced water. Using a 2 in. (5 cm) diameter cookie cutter, cut into disks, then cut each in half to make half-moons.

TO SERVE

Using a 2 3/4 in. (7 cm) diameter presentation ring, juxtapose the gelatin half-moons, alternating with the fish strips and radishes. Continue to fill the ring to form a rosette. Carefully transfer to a plate and remove the ring. Add a few dots of yuzu jelly on top, then season with a drizzle of kaffir lime leaf oil and a little fleur de sel. Finish by pouring the citrus bouillon around the edge.

ROOTS —— WINTER P. 62

FISH OF THE DAY AND **LEEKS**

SERVES 4

FOR THE FISH
2 gurnard fillets
(or other sustainable fish
from your region)
1 tsp. (5 g) Guérande unrefined sea salt
4 tsp. (20 g) clarified butter,
for brushing
A few grains of fleur de sel

FOR THE LEEK VEIL
8 3/4 oz. (250 g) large leeks
Olive oil

FOR THE LEEK BUTTER
4 1/2 oz. (125 g) leek leaves
(from the leeks used for the veil)
1/2 cup (125 ml) clarified butter

FOR THE BÉARNAISE
1/3 cup + 1 1/2 tbsp. (100 ml) white wine
Scant 1/4 cup (50 ml) white wine vinegar
3 tbsp. (10 g) chopped tarragon
2 tbsp. finely chopped shallot
1 3/4 tsp. (5 g) black peppercorns
3 egg yolks
4 tsp. (20 ml) lemon juice
4 tsp. (20 ml) water
1/2 tsp. unrefined sea salt
1/3 cup + 1 1/2 tbsp. (100 ml)
clarified leek butter (see above)

FOR THE FISH

Season the fish with a fine layer of Guérande salt and let rest for 12 hours in the refrigerator so that the salt dries the flesh and removes any excess water.
Cook the fish in a combi oven at 167°F (75°C) with 10% humidity for 8–12 minutes (cooking time will depend on the thickness of the fillet). Using a knife, cut the fillet into 1 1/4 in. (3 cm) thick portions. Brush with the clarified butter and season with a few grains of fleur de sel.

FOR THE LEEK VEIL

Preheat the oven to 380°F (195°C/gas 5). Trim the roots and leaves (the green parts) from the leeks. Reserve the leaves for the leek butter. Wash the leeks, then cook them in the oven for 25–30 minutes. The exterior should be burned and the inside well cooked. Cut the leeks in half lengthwise and remove the outer leaves (two or three layers). Open out the interior leaves on the work surface.
Lay the leek leaves on top of each other, half overlapping them. Cut out rectangles of about 5 x 2 3/4 in. (12 x 7 cm). Using a kitchen blowtorch, brown them on one side, then set aside on a piece of parchment (baking) paper of the same size. Brush with the olive oil.
Reheat in a steam oven at 185°F (85°C) and peel off the paper to serve.

FOR THE LEEK BUTTER

Wash the reserved leek greens and cut them into pieces. In a Thermomix®, mix them with the clarified butter on high speed for 1 minute, then lower the speed to 2/4 and let infuse at 205°F (95°C) for 25 minutes. Strain through a chinois without pressing too hard. Store the butter in the refrigerator.

FOR THE BÉARNAISE

In a saucepan, reduce the wine, vinegar, tarragon, shallot, and pepper by half. Strain and reserve.
Place the egg yolks in a skillet (frying pan) with the lemon juice, water, and unrefined sea salt. Add the wine and vinegar reduction. Heat gently, while whisking vigorously to stir in air, until the eggs are cooked but creamy. Remove from the heat and gradually stir in the clarified leek butter. Add a little water if necessary. Taste and season with more salt if needed. The sauce should be quite runny.
Transfer to a siphon fitted with two gas cartridges. Keep the béarnaise warm.

FOR THE BLACK GARLIC PURÉE

3 1/2 oz. (100 g) black garlic (2 heads)
1 3/4 oz. (50 g) white garlic (1 head)
4 1/4 cups (1 L) cold water
1/3 cup (80 ml) whole milk
Scant 1/4 cup (50 ml) water
2 tbsp. squid ink
Salt

FOR THE MUSSEL AND TOASTED YEAST SAUCE

2 shallots, finely chopped
4 tsp. (20 ml) olive oil
1/3 oz. (10 g) parsley (1/4 cup chopped)
1 lb. 2 oz. (500 g) mussels
3 1/2 oz. (100 g) nutritional yeast shavings
2 tbsp. butter
1/3 cup + 1 1/2 tbsp. (100 ml) white wine
Scant 1/4 cup (50 ml) whipping cream
1/2 tsp. unrefined sea salt

FOR THE BLACK GARLIC PURÉE

Peel the black garlic heads. Peel the white garlic and remove the germ from the cloves.

Put 4 1/4 cups (1 L) water in a saucepan with the white garlic and bring to a boil. Once it has reached boiling point, strain through a chinois and return the garlic to the pan with fresh water. Boil and strain again. Repeat this process five times, starting with cold water each time.

In another saucepan, gently heat the black garlic, cooked white garlic, milk, and a scant 1/4 cup (50 ml) water until the mixture is dry, about 15 minutes.

Mix to a smooth purée in a blender. Add the squid ink and blend again. Add a little salt if needed.

FOR THE MUSSEL AND TOASTED YEAST SAUCE

Preheat the oven to 320°F (160°C/gas 3). In a large saucepan, sweat half the chopped shallot in the olive oil with the parsley without browning it. Once the shallot is soft, add the mussels, cover the pan and let cook over low heat for 20 minutes. When all the mussels have opened, strain through a chinois and reserve the liquid. Set aside.

Toast the yeast in the oven for 5 minutes. Set aside.

In another saucepan, sweat the remaining chopped shallot with the butter. Deglaze with the white wine and let the alcohol evaporate. Add the mussel cooking liquid and simmer for 5 minutes. Stir in the cream and simmer for 1 minute. Remove from the heat and strain.

Stir in the toasted yeast, then mix well using an immersion blender. Season with unrefined sea salt.

TO SERVE

Add a dot of black garlic purée in the center of a dish. Place the cooked fish on top and add 2 tablespoons of the toasted yeast sauce around the edge. Place the béarnaise on top of the fish, then cover with the leek veil.

SUNCHOKE CHURROS

SERVES 6

FOR THE CHURRO BATTER
1 cup (240 ml) milk
1/3 cup + 1 1/2 tbsp. (100 g) butter, diced
2 1/2 tsp. (1/3 oz./10 g) superfine (caster) sugar
1/4 tsp. unrefined sea salt
1/3 tsp. vanilla extract
3/4 cup (3 1/2 oz./100 g) flour
6 1/2 oz. (180 g) eggs
Sunflower oil

FOR THE SUNCHOKE (JERUSALEM ARTICHOKE) POWDER
7 oz. (200 g) sunchokes (Jerusalem artichokes)

FOR THE SUNCHOKE (JERUSALEM ARTICHOKE) SUGAR
1 cup (7 oz./200 g) superfine (caster) sugar
3/4 cup (3 1/2 oz./100 g) powdered sunchoke (Jerusalem artichoke)

FOR THE SUNCHOKE (JERUSALEM ARTICHOKE) DULCE DE LECHE
1 2/3 cups (1 lb. 2 oz./500 g) dulce de leche
6 1/4 oz. (175 g) sunchoke (Jerusalem artichoke) flesh

FOR THE CHURRO BATTER

In a saucepan, heat the milk with the butter, sugar, salt, and vanilla extract. When it comes to a boil, add the flour and whisk to prevent lumps forming. Pour the mixture into the bowl of a stand mixer fitted with the paddle attachment and beat gently until the batter has cooled slightly. Then add the eggs, one at a time. Transfer the batter to a pastry (piping) bag fitted with a fluted tip (nozzle). Pipe the batter in small root shapes onto a silicone baking mat, then refrigerate to harden.

FOR THE SUNCHOKE (JERUSALEM ARTICHOKE) POWDER

Clean the sunchokes (Jerusalem artichokes) and wrap them separately in foil. Cook in the oven at 360°F (180°C/gas 4) for 40 minutes. Once they are well cooked, remove the foil and let cool slightly. Cut them in half and reserve the flesh. Set aside in the refrigerator.
Dry the sunchoke skins in a desiccator for 8 hours, then blend to a fine powder.

FOR THE SUNCHOKE (JERUSALEM ARTICHOKE) SUGAR

In a bowl, stir together the sugar and the sunchoke powder.

TO COOK THE CHURROS

Fry the churros in oil at 355°F (180°C). Sprinkle liberally with the sunchoke sugar.

FOR THE SUNCHOKE (JERUSALEM ARTICHOKE) DULCE DE LECHE

In a Thermomix®, blend the dulce de leche with the reserved cooked sunchoke flesh. Set aside at room temperature.

TO SERVE

Fill a dish with twigs, then arrange the sunchoke churros on top. Serve the dulce de leche separately in a little pot.

ROOTS —— WINTER P. 68

CELTUCE, STRACCIATELLA, AND CAVIAR

SERVES 4

FOR THE CELTUCE

1 lb. 2 oz. (500 g) celtuce
1 2/3 cups (400 ml) water
1/2 tsp. ascorbic acid

TO SERVE

4 1/4 oz. (120 g) stracciatella di bufala
2 1/2 tbsp. Ossetra caviar
1/3 cup (75 ml) whipping cream
2 tsp. green herb oil (see page 265)
Fleur de sel

FOR THE CELTUCE

Using a mandoline, cut the celtuce into slices lengthwise. Cut shapes from these slices using small and large flower-shaped cookie (pastry) cutters. Set aside in the cold water with the ascorbic acid.

TO SERVE

Shape the stracciatella into 1 oz. (30 g) balls.
Using a melon baller, form 1/3 oz. (10 g) balls from the caviar.
Place four 2 in. (5 cm) diameter circles on a baking sheet lined with parchment (baking) paper. Place a stracciatella ball in the center of each circle and top with a ball of caviar. Drain the celtuce "petals" and carefully arrange them around the outside, forming a "flower." Juxtapose the small "petals" on the inside with the larger ones on the outside. Add three rings of petals to create a beautiful flower, then carefully transfer the flower to the dish and remove the circle.
Place a tablespoon of cream around the edge and add a few drops of the green oil and a few grains of fleur de sel.

GARDEN SALAD
AND VERMOUTH SAUCE

SERVES 4

FOR THE SALAD
2 small heads of lettuce (Little Gem, salanova butterhead, curly endive)
Olive oil
Herb oil (see page 265)
Fleur de sel

FOR THE VERMOUTH SAUCE
Scant 1/4 cup (1 oz./30 g) finely chopped shallot
1 1/2 tbsp. (3/4 oz./20 g) butter
1 cup + 1 tbsp. (250 ml) dry white vermouth
1/2 cup (125 ml) white wine
2 cups + 2 tbsp. (500 ml) cream
5/8 cup (150 ml) shellfish jus
Unrefined sea salt

FOR THE TOKYO TURNIP LEAVES
1 cup + 1 tbsp. (250 ml) cider vinegar
1/3 cup (75 ml) water
1/4 cup (1 3/4 oz./50 g) superfine (caster) sugar
1 Tokyo turnip

FOR THE HERB MIX
12 chickweed sprouts
12 garden burnet sprouts
12 fennel fronds
12 baby arugula (rocket) sprouts
12 baby nasturtium sprouts
6 fresh almonds

FOR THE SALAD

Cut the lettuces in half and wash and dry them with paper towels. Heat a drizzle of olive oil in a skillet (frying pan). Brown the lettuces on both sides without overcooking them. Brush them with the herb oil and season with a few grains of fleur de sel.

FOR THE VERMOUTH SAUCE

In a small saucepan, sweat the chopped shallot in the butter. Add the vermouth and wine and reduce by half. Then, stir in the cream and shellfish jus. Cook over low heat until creamy (the sauce should be reduced by almost half). Season with unrefined sea salt. Strain and keep warm.

FOR THE TOKYO TURNIP LEAVES

Pour the vinegar, water, and sugar into a saucepan and bring to a boil, then turn off the heat and let cool.
Using a mandoline, cut the turnip into very thin (2 mm) slices. Cut out little leaves using a shaped cookie (pastry) cutter. Set aside half in cold water. Place the other half into the prepared brine.

FOR THE HERB MIX

Thoroughly wash and dry the herbs. Divide the herbs between four glasses and set aside in the refrigerator.
Crack the fresh almonds and separate them into halves. Set aside in cold water.

TO SERVE

Place the salad in the center of a dish. Place the raw and pickled Tokyo turnip leaves between the salad leaves, adding volume. Tuck the almonds between the leaves. Arrange the herb mix on top of the salad. Finish by pouring the warm vermouth sauce around the salad.

LEAVES —— SPRING P. 76

GREEN TEA AND BABY SQUID

SERVES 4

FOR THE CHARD AND GREEN TEA STUFFING

2 3/4 oz. (80 g) chard leaves
2 3/4 oz. (80 g) spinach leaves
1 1/2 tbsp. (1/3 oz./10 g) finely chopped shallot
1/2 cup (2 3/4 oz./75 g) spinach purée
4 tsp. (1/2 oz./15 g) grated Parmesan
1/2 tbsp. (4 g) dried genmaicha tea leaves
2 tsp. (5 g) black nori powder
1 1/2 tsp. (1/4 oz./8 g) yellow miso
1 tsp. colatura di alici (Italian fermented anchovy sauce)
Zest of 1 untreated lemon
Olive oil
Unrefined sea salt

FOR THE BABY SQUID

12 baby squid
4 tsp. (3/4 oz./20 g) clarified butter

FOR THE GENMAICHA SAUCE

1 cup + 1 tbsp. (250 ml) water
1 oz. (25 g) royal kombu
1 oz. (25 g) dried squid
2 sticks + 2 tbsp. (8 3/4 oz./250 g) cold butter
2 tsp. (5 g) dried genmaicha tea leaves
1 tbsp. (10 g) matcha powder
3 1/2 tbsp. (50 ml) whipping cream
Unrefined sea salt

TO SERVE

3 tbsp. (3/4 oz./20 g) dried genmaicha tea leaves
Olive oil

FOR THE CHARD AND GREEN TEA STUFFING

Fill a saucepan with water and bring to a boil with a pinch of unrefined sea salt. Add the chard and spinach leaves and blanch for 1 minute. Drain and transfer the leaves to iced water and let cool. Drain, then chop the leaves as finely as possible. In a skillet (frying pan), sweat the shallot in a drizzle of olive oil. Once softened, let the shallot cool, then chop as finely as possible.
Transfer the chopped leaves and shallot to a bowl and stir in the remaining ingredients. Season to taste with unrefined sea salt. Transfer the mixture to a pastry (piping) bag.

FOR THE BABY SQUID

Clean the baby squid, using as little water as possible, removing the eyes, beak, viscera, quill, ink sac, and any sand remaining inside. Separate the head from the body.
Stuff each baby squid with the chard and green tea stuffing. Secure by tying their tentacles, then cook in a steam oven at 185°F (85°C) for 2 minutes. Once cooked, brush them with clarified butter before serving.

FOR THE GENMAICHA SAUCE

Put the water into a saucepan and stir in the kombu and dried squid. Cover the pan, heat to 140°F (60°C), and cook for 2 hours.
Strain and reserve the cooking liquid. Use it to make a *beurre monté* in a saucepan over low heat. Dice the cold butter and add to the pan, whisking continuously. Add the genmaicha and let infuse for 5 minutes (no longer or the sauce will become bitter), remove the leaves.
In a small bowl, stir the matcha powder into the cream. Just before serving, heat a little *beurre monté* and add 1 tablespoon of the matcha cream. Season with salt.

TO SERVE

Sort through the genmaicha tea leaves, setting aside the small grains of puffed rice. Pour a little of the genmaicha sauce into the bottom of a dish. Arrange three baby squid next to each other on top.
Add a few grains of puffed rice and a few drops of olive oil around them.

LEAVES —— SPRING P. 78

FENNEL, VANILLA, AND WHITE CHOCOLATE

SERVES 4

FOR THE SABLÉS
1/3 cup + 2 tbsp. (3 1/2 oz./100 g) butter
1/2 cup (3 1/2 oz./100 g) demerara sugar
Scant 1 cup (5 oz./150 g) rice flour
1/3 cup + 2 tsp. (1 3/4 oz./50 g) cornstarch (cornflour)
1/2 tsp. (3 g) unrefined sea salt
4 1/2 oz. (130 g) white couverture chocolate
1/2 cup + 1 tbsp. (4 1/2 oz./130 g) cocoa butter

FOR THE CANDIED FENNEL
1 1/4 cups (8 3/4 oz./250 g) superfine (caster) sugar
1 cup + 1 tbsp. (250 ml) water
1 star anise
1 fennel bulb

FOR THE FENNEL SORBET
5 oz. (150 g) fennel
1 1/4 cups (300 ml) water
1/3 cup + 1 tbsp. (2 3/4 oz./80 g) superfine (caster) sugar
1/4 cup + 1 tbsp. (1 oz./30 g) glucose powder
2 3/4 tbsp. pastis

FOR THE VANILLA WHIPPED CREAM
4 1/4 cups (1 L) whipping cream
5 vanilla beans (pods)
1 1/4 cups (1 1/2 oz./300 g) mascarpone
1/3 cup + 2 tbsp. (3 1/4 oz./90 g) superfine (caster) sugar

FOR THE FENNEL PETALS
1 fennel bulb

FOR THE FENNEL "OSMOSIS"
1 fennel bulb
3 1/2 cups (1 lb. 9 oz./700 g) superfine (caster) sugar
3 cups (700 ml) water
4 vanilla beans (pods)

FOR THE VANILLA OIL
5 vanilla beans (pods)
2 cups + 2 tbsp. (500 ml) sunflower oil

TO SERVE
Fennel fronds

FOR THE SABLÉS

Preheat the oven to 320°F (160°C/gas 3). In a mixer, mix the butter with the demerara sugar. Add the flour, cornstarch (cornflour), and salt and mix until the ingredients are just combined. Pour the mixture onto a baking sheet covered with a silicone baking mat and bake in the oven for 12 minutes. Remove from the oven and crumble using your hands.

In a small saucepan, melt the white couverture chocolate and the cocoa butter, then add the biscuit crumbs and mix using a rubber spatula. Spread the mixture onto the silicone baking mat again, pressing it down well with a spatula. Refrigerate for 2 hours then cut into 1/2 in. (1 cm) squares.

FOR THE CANDIED FENNEL

In a saucepan, boil the sugar and water with the star anise for 15 minutes to obtain a syrup. Cut the fennel into thick slices and cook them in the syrup for about 40 minutes, then let cool in the refrigerator.

FOR THE FENNEL SORBET

Finely slice the fennel then blend it with the water. Strain, pressing down. In a saucepan, make a syrup with the fennel liquid, sugar, and glucose powder. Let cool, then stir in the pastis. Pour into a Pacojet®, freeze, and pacotize.

FOR THE VANILLA WHIPPED CREAM

In a saucepan, heat the cream with the split and scraped vanilla beans (pods). Let infuse for 10 minutes, then add the mascarpone and the sugar and mix. Let mature in the refrigerator for 24 hours, then lightly whip.

FOR THE FENNEL PETALS

Separate the layers of the fennel and, using a cookie (pastry) cutter, cut them into petal shapes. Place them immediately into iced water and set aside.

FOR THE FENNEL "OSMOSIS"

Using a mandoline, thinly slice the fennel. Make a syrup with the sugar, water, and split and scraped vanilla beans. Once the syrup is cold, infuse the fennel in the syrup then place in a sous-vide machine to absorb some of the syrup.

FOR THE VANILLA OIL

Split the vanilla beans and scrape the seeds into the oil, then blend with the beans using an immersion blender. Pour into a small saucepan and heat to 122°F (50°C), then let infuse for 30 minutes. Strain, then transfer to a pipette.

TO SERVE

Arrange a few cubes of candied fennel in a dish, add some pieces of sablé, and a few drops of vanilla oil. Place a quenelle of fennel sorbet in the center, then cover everything with the vanilla whipped cream. Finish by decorating with the fennel petals, a few fennel fronds, and the fennel "osmosis."

LEAVES —— SPRING P. 80

MALABAR SPINACH
AND FISH TARTARE

SERVES 4

FOR THE TAPIOCA CRISPS
4 1/4 cups (1 L) water
1/3 cup (1 3/4 oz./50 g) Japanese pearl tapioca
1/4 oz. (5 g) fisherman's salad (mix of dried seaweed flakes)
4 1/4 cups (1 L) sunflower oil
Unrefined sea salt

FOR THE FISH TARTARE
3 1/2 oz. (100 g) bonito (or other sustainable fish from your region)
2 tsp. (1/3 oz./10 g) seed-style mustard
4 tsp. (20 ml) extra virgin olive oil
1/2 tsp. unrefined sea salt
1 tbsp. lemon juice
Zest of 1/2 lemon
Zest of 1/2 lime

FOR THE PONZU GEL
1 cup + 1 tbsp. (250 ml) ponzu
Scant 1/4 cup (50 ml) dashi
4 tsp. (1/4 oz./8 g) agar-agar powder

FOR THE KAFFIR LIME MAYONNAISE
2 egg yolks
1/3 cup + 1 1/2 tbsp. (100 ml) kaffir lime leaf oil (see page 219)
A few drops of lemon juice
Pinch of unrefined sea salt

TO SERVE
12 Malabar spinach leaves

FOR THE TAPIOCA CRISPS

Bring the water to a boil in a saucepan, add salt, and pour in the tapioca. Let boil for 15 minutes. It needs to be well cooked. Drain and stir together with the fisherman's salad.
Spread evenly in a very thin (2 mm) layer onto a silicone baking mat. Let dry in the oven at 45°F (70°C) for about 2 hours.
Fry the tapioca in the sunflower oil at 390°F (200°C), then divide into pieces of about 2–2 1/2 in. (5–6 cm) square.

FOR THE FISH TARTARE

Finely chop the fish and season with the remaining ingredients.

FOR THE PONZU GEL

Place the ponzu, dashi, and agar-agar in a saucepan and bring to a boil. Boil for 2 minutes, stirring constantly. Remove from the heat, spread out onto a baking sheet, and let cool. Once the gel is set and cold, blend it. Transfer to a pipette and set aside in the refrigerator.

FOR THE KAFFIR LIME MAYONNAISE

Mix the eggs using an immersion blender, gradually drizzling in the oil. Season with the lemon juice and salt. Transfer to a pipette and set aside in the refrigerator.

TO SERVE

Place a good spoonful of fish tartare on each of the tapioca crisps.
Garnish with a few dots of the ponzu gel and kaffir lime mayonnaise. Cover with the Malabar spinach leaves.

LEAVES —— SUMMER P. 83

NEW ZEALAND SPINACH
AND SQUID

SERVES 4

FOR THE SQUID

1 large squid (at least 2 1/4 lb./1 kg)
Olive oil
Fleur de sel

FOR THE GREEN CURRY SAUCE

2 3/4 oz. (75 g) fresh ginger
1 oz. (25 g) fresh galangal
2 1/4 oz. (60 g) lemongrass (about 3 stalks)
1 oz. (25 g) garlic
2 tsp. (1/3 oz./10 g) coriander seeds
1 star anise
3 cardamom pods
3/4 oz. (20 g) fresh turmeric root
2 3/4 oz. (80 g) carrot
1 3/4 oz. (50 g) shallot
2 oz. (55 g) scallion (spring onion), white parts
1 1/2 oz. (40 g) celery
1 chile pepper
1 1/2 oz. (40 g) tamarind
7/8 cup (200 ml) dashi or shellfish stock
2 cups + 2 tbsp. (500 ml) whipping cream
Zest of 3 limes
2 1/4 oz. (60 g) scallion (spring onion), green parts
1 oz. (30 g) cilantro (fresh coriander) (2/3 cup chopped)
2 1/4 oz. (60 g) Granny Smith apple
Juice of 2 limes
Grapeseed oil

FOR THE GARNISHES

1 Granny Smith apple
Ascorbic acid
1 celery stalk
20 New Zealand spinach leaves

FOR THE LIME GEL

1 cup (250 ml) lime juice
3 1/2 tsp. (1/4 oz./7 g) agar-agar powder

FOR THE SQUID

Clean the squid and remove the tentacles. Cut the tubes down one side and remove the inner and outer skin, then flatten and freeze them. Cut the frozen squid into 1 1/2–2 1/2 in. (4–6 cm) rectangles. In a skillet (frying pan), sear over high heat in a drizzle of olive oil, then, cut lengthwise into 1/4 in. (5 mm) thick slices. Finish cooking gently in the salamander. Season with a few grains of fleur de sel. Keep warm.

FOR THE GREEN CURRY SAUCE

Peel and finely chop all the ingredients, keeping them separate.
In a saucepan, sweat the ginger and galangal in plenty of grapeseed oil. Add the lemongrass and garlic, then the coriander seeds, star anise, and the seeds from the cardamom pods. Stir, then add the turmeric and carrot and continue cooking for 10 minutes over high heat, adding a little water if sticking.
Next, add the shallot, scallion (spring onion) whites, celery, chile pepper, and tamarind. Stir, then pour in the dashi, cream, and lime zest and let cook over low heat for an additional 15 minutes. Finally, remove from the heat and stir in the scallion greens, the cilantro (fresh coriander), and the apple.
Blend everything in a blender for 1–2 minutes on maximum speed, then strain through a chinois. Season with the lime juice to add acidity and freshness.

FOR THE GARNISHES

Peel, core, and slice the apple, reserving the trimmings. Cut the slices into sticks the same size as the squid. Using a juicer, make a juice from the peel and core (adding a little ascorbic acid). Immerse the apple strips in the juice and place in a sous-vide machine until the apple sticks have absorbed all the juice. They should be transparent.
Wash the celery, then cut it diagonally into very thin (2 mm) slices. Set aside in iced water.

FOR THE LIME GEL

In a saucepan, boil the lime juice with the agar-agar for 2 minutes, while whisking continuously. Let cool, then blend. Transfer to a pipette and set aside.

TO SERVE

Arrange the squid and green apple sticks in a small dish, alternating them and placing them side by side in a row. Add a second layer, then move everything carefully to the left of the dish. Add five dots of lime gel and place a piece of celery on top of each dot. Top the squid with five New Zealand spinach leaves. Finish with a spoonful of green curry sauce around the edge.

FISH OF THE DAY AND **SHISO**

SERVES 4

FOR THE FERMENTED SHISO LEAVES
8 large red shiso leaves
2 tbsp. white balsamic vinegar
Pinch of unrefined sea salt

FOR THE FISH
1 John Dory fillet
(or other sustainable fish
from your region)

FOR THE SAKE SAUCE
1 3/4 tbsp. (1 oz./25 g) sushi rice
1/3 cup + 1 1/2 tbsp. (100 ml) fish stock
1 3/4 sticks (7 oz./200 g) cold butter, diced
3 tbsp. (1 oz./25 g) rice koji
2 tsp. yellow miso
1 tbsp. sake
1/2 tbsp. (1/3 oz./10 g) sake kasu
Unrefined sea salt

FOR THE SHISO GEL
1 1/4 cups (300 ml) water
1 oz. (30 g) red shiso leaves
2/3 tsp. (2.5 g) superfine (caster) sugar
Scant 4 tsp. (7.5 g) agar-agar powder
Pinch of citric acid
1/8 tsp. (0.5 g) red miso
1/5 oz. (5 g) *umeboshi*
(salted Japanese plum)

FOR THE FERMENTED SHISO LEAVES

Place the red shiso leaves in a sous-vide bag and stir in the vinegar and salt. Seal and let ferment for 3 days at room temperature.
Once the shiso leaves are ready, store in the refrigerator.

FOR THE FISH

Cook the fish fillet, skin side down, in a combi oven at 165°F (75°C) with 10% humidity for 8 minutes.
Cut the fish into 3/4 in. (2 cm) slices. Cover each portion with half a fermented shiso leaf.

FOR THE SAKE SAUCE

Toast the sushi rice in a skillet (frying pan) over low heat. Set aside.
In a saucepan, reduce the fish stock by half. Gradually whisk in the diced butter to make a *beurre monté*. Add the toasted rice and the rice koji. Let infuse for 30 minutes. Strain through a chinois, then season with the yellow miso, sake, and sake kasu. Adjust the seasoning with unrefined sea salt. Keep warm.

FOR THE SHISO GEL

Put the water and shiso leaves in a saucepan and bring to a boil. Blend, then strain through a Superbag® back into the saucepan. Stir in the sugar and agar-agar and boil for 2 minutes, then transfer to a stainless-steel container and let cool.
Blend with the citric acid, red miso, *umeboshi*, and the water from the fermented shiso leaf sachet. Transfer to a pipette and set aside in the refrigerator.

TO SERVE

Arrange the fish and shiso leaf in a dish.
Add a dot of shiso get on one side and the sake sauce on the other side.

LEAVES —— SUMMER P. 88

DULSE SEAWEED AND CHERRIES

SERVES 4

FOR THE CHERRY JUICE

1 lb. 2 oz. (500 g) pitted (stoned) cherries (Napoleon or Bigarreau, if available)
1/2 cup + 1 tbsp. (4 oz./110 g) superfine (caster) sugar
1 cup + 1 tbsp. (250 ml) water
1 tsp. citric acid

FOR THE POACHED CHERRIES

8 3/4 oz. (250 g) cherries
Scant 1/4 cup (50 ml) cherry juice

FOR THE DULSE SEAWEED ICE CREAM

1 cup + 2 tbsp. (280 ml) whole milk
1/3 cup (86 ml) whipping cream
1/2 cup less 1 tbsp. (2 1/2 oz./70 g) dextrose
3 tbsp. (3/4 oz./21 g) low-fat (semi-skimmed) powdered milk
2 tsp. (1/2 oz./13 g) inverted sugar syrup
2 tbsp. (1 oz./25 g) superfine (caster) sugar
2 1/2 tsp. (6 g) carob flour
1 1/2 oz. (40 g) desalted fresh dulse seaweed, chopped
15 pieces of dried dulse seaweed, crushed

FOR THE "CLAFOUTIS" VEIL

3 1/2 oz. (100 g) eggs
1 cup + 2 1/2 tbsp. (8 oz./225 g) superfine (caster) sugar
5/8 cup (150 ml) olive oil
1/2 tsp. (2.5 g) unrefined sea salt
3/4 cup + 1 tbsp. (3 1/2 oz./100 g) pastry (soft) flour
1/2 tsp. (2 g) baking soda (bicarbonate of soda)
1/2 tsp.(1.5 g) baking powder
3/4 cup (175 ml) almond milk
1/4 cup (60 ml) orange juice
2 3/4 tbsp. cherry brandy
4 tsp. (20 ml) amaretto

FOR THE SEAWEED OPALINE

1 1/4 cups (8 3/4 oz./250 g) superfine (caster) sugar
1 lb. 2 oz. (500 g) fondant
Scant 3/4 cup (8 3/4 oz./250 g) glucose syrup
1 3/4 oz. (50 g) dried dulse seaweed

FOR THE CHERRY JUICE

Place all the ingredients in a saucepan and bring to a boil. Blend, then strain through a chinois and set aside the juice.

FOR THE POACHED CHERRIES

Cut the cherries in half and remove the pits (stones). Place the cherries in a saucepan and cover them with the cherry juice. Cook over low heat for 30 minutes. Remove from the heat, let cool and set aside in the refrigerator.

FOR THE DULSE SEAWEED ICE CREAM

In a saucepan, heat the milk, cream, dextrose, powdered milk, and inverted sugar syrup to 104°F (40°C). Stir in the sugar and carob flour. Keep heating until the temperature reaches 180°F (82°C), then stir in the fresh and dried seaweed. Remove from the heat and let cool to 39°F (4°C). Chill for several hours in the refrigerator. The next day, strain through a Superbag®, then churn in an ice cream maker.

FOR THE "CLAFOUTIS" VEIL

In a stand mixer, whisk the eggs with the sugar. Once mixture is foamy, gradually drizzle in the olive oil to obtain an emulsion. Sift the dry ingredients (the pastry/soft flour, baking soda/bicarbonate of soda, and baking powder) into another bowl, then gradually add them to the egg mixture, alternating with the liquids (the almond milk, orange juice, cherry brandy, and amaretto).
Line a stainless-steel lidded baking pan with a silicone baking mat of the same size. Spread 7 oz. (200 g) of the mixture into the pan in an even layer. Cover the pan with a lid and cook in a steam oven at 250°F (120°C) for 9 minutes. Remove the lid, then cook in a dry oven at 285°F (140°C/gas 1) for 3 minutes. Unmold and, using a cookie (pastry) cutter, cut out 6 in. (15 cm) diameter disks. Set aside in the refrigerator.

FOR THE SEAWEED OPALINE

Preheat the oven to 375°F (190°C/gas 5). Prepare the dry caramel. Heat the sugar in a skillet (frying pan) until colored. Pour onto a silicone baking mat and let cool at room temperature. In a saucepan, heat the fondant and glucose syrup, then stir in 8 3/4 oz. (250 g) of the dry caramel. Pour onto a silicone baking mat and let cool. Once cool, blend to a fine powder. Line a baking sheet with a silicone baking mat, then sift the opaline in a thin layer over the surface. Add the dulse seaweed on top. Cook in the oven for 3 minutes, then turn off the oven and leave the opaline in the oven until it has dissolved. Remove from the oven, carefully remove it from the tray, and let cool. Store in an airtight container.

LEAVES —— SUMMER P. 90

FOR THE CHERRY POWDER
3 1/2 oz. (100 g) cherries

FOR THE CHERRY "JUS LIÉ"
1/3 cup + 1 1/2 tbsp. (100 ml) cherry juice (see left)
4 tsp. (20 ml) water
1/4 tsp. citric acid
Scant 1/8 tsp. (0.2 g) xanthan gum

FOR THE KIRSCH BEER JELLY
4 gold gelatin leaves (8 g)
3/8 cup (90 ml) water
1 cup + 1 tbsp. (250 ml) kirsch beer

FOR THE SABLÉS
1 cup (8 oz./225 g) butter, softened
3/4 cup + 1 1/4 tbsp. (6 1/2 oz./180 g) demerara sugar
1/3 cup + 1 tbsp. (2 3/4 oz./75 g) superfine (caster) sugar
1 tsp. (4.5 g) fleur de sel
2 1/2 cups (1[illegible] oz./305 g) all-purpose (plain) flour
1 3/4 tsp. (1/4 oz./7.5 g) baking soda (bicarbonate of soda)
2 cups (8 oz./225 g) slivered (flaked) almonds
5 oz. (150 g) white chocolate
1/3 cup + 2 tbsp. (3 1/2 oz./100 g) cocoa butter

FOR THE SEA LETTUCE CRISTALLINES
3 1/2 oz. (100 g) fresh sea lettuce
Sunflower oil

FOR THE CHERRY POWDER

Wash and pit the cherries. Spread them out on a baking sheet, then dry them in a desiccator at 122°F (50°C) for 12 hours or overnight. Once the cherries are dried, blend them to fine powder.

FOR THE CHERRY "JUS LIÉ"

Stir together the cherry juice, water, and citric acid. Add the xanthan gum, then blend. Remove the air in a sous-vide machine.

FOR THE KIRSCH BEER JELLY

Soak the gelatin leaves in iced water to hydrate. In a saucepan, boil the water. Remove from the heat and stir in the gelatin until dissolved. Add the beer and mix well. Pour the mixture into a stainless-steel container and let cool in the refrigerator.

FOR THE SABLÉS

In a stand mixer fitted with the paddle attachment, beat the butter with the sugars and fleur de sel, then sift in the flour and baking soda. Continue mixing until smooth, then stir in the slivered (flaked) almonds. Roll the dough out thinly (5 mm) onto a baking sheet and set aside in the refrigerator for 12 hours or overnight.
Preheat the oven to 340°F (170°C/gas 4). Cut the rolled-out dough into small (1/5 in./5 mm) cubes and bake in the oven for about 13 minutes, then let cool.
In a saucepan, melt the white chocolate with the cocoa butter. Dip the sablé cubes in the chocolate, then drain on a wire rack. When set, place in the refrigerator.

FOR THE SEA LETTUCE CRISTALLINES

Desalt the sea lettuce in fresh water. Spread it out on a silicone baking mat, then place it in a desiccator at 131°F (55°F) for 24 hours. Carefully lift it from the silicone baking mat, then fry it briefly in the sunflower oil heated to 284°F (140°C).

TO SERVE

Place a tablespoon of the poached cherries into a dish. Add a few sablé cubes and some kirsch beer jelly next to it. Pour two tablespoons of the cherry "jus lié" around the edge. Then, place a quenelle of the dulse seaweed ice cream in the center. Cover everything with the "clafoutis" veil. Top with a piece of the seaweed opaline, then melt it using a kitchen blowtorch. Sprinkle with the cherry powder and decorate with some sea lettuce cristallines.

LEAVES —— SUMMER P. 90

SAGE AND COMTÉ CANNELÉ

MAKES 35 CANNELÉS

FOR THE CANNELÉ MIXTURE
4 1/2 oz. (125 g) Comté cheese 36 months (1 cup + 2 tbsp. grated)
3 1/2 oz. (100 g) whole eggs
1 1/2 oz. (40 g) egg yolk
Scant 1/4 cup (1 3/4 oz./50 g) butter
2 cups + 2 tbsp. (500 ml) whole milk
Scant 2/3 cup (4 1/2 oz./125 g) isomalt
1/2 tsp. (3.5 g) salt
3/4 cup (3 1/2 oz./100 g) flour

FOR THE COMTÉ AND SAGE CREAM
3/4 oz. (20 g) sage leaves
3/4 cup + 1 tbsp. (200 ml) whipping cream
5 oz. (150 g) Comté cheese 36 months (1 1/3 cups grated)

FOR THE CANNELÉ MIXTURE

Place all the ingredients except the flour in a Thermomix®. Mix on medium speed (speed 2) at 122°F (50°C) for 15 minutes. Once the Comté has melted, add the flour and mix for 2 minutes on high speed (speed 6). Pour the mixture into a bowl and let cool in the refrigerator overnight.
Half fill silicone cannelé molds with the cannelé mixture. Cook in a steam oven, fan 2, at 205°F (95°C) for 30 minutes. Finish cooking in a dry oven at 205°F (95°C) with 100% humidity and no fan for 15 minutes. Let cool at room temperature for 10 minutes.
Once the cannelés are lukewarm, return them to the dry oven and cook at 375°F (190°C/gas 5), fan 4, for 10 minutes. Let rest at room temperature for 5 minutes, then return to the oven for 20 minutes. Unmold onto a cooling rack.

FOR THE COMTÉ AND SAGE CREAM

Blanch the sage leaves in a saucepan of boiling water for 7 minutes. Heat the cream and blend in the Thermomix® with the Comté and the blanched sage. Let cool at room temperature then strain through a sieve.
Transfer the cream to a pastry (piping) bag fitted with a thin tip (nozzle) or to a pipette so that you can fill the cannelés. It is important not to leave the cream in the refrigerator or it may separate.

TO SERVE

Make a small hole in the base of each cannelé and fill with the Comté and sage cream.

OYSTER AND **CODIUM**

SERVES 4

FOR THE OYSTERS
4 Gillardeau oysters, size no. 2
8 large bay leaves

FOR THE CODIUM BUTTER
3 1/2 oz. (100 g) codium (seaweed)
1/3 cup + 2 tbsp. (3 1/2 oz./100 g) butter

TO PREPARE AND COOK THE OYSTERS

Carefully open the oysters. Strain the water from the oysters through a sieve twice and use this filtered water to clean the oyster and remove any impurities. Reserve the shells for presentation.
Place each oyster between two bay leaves and cook on a charcoal grill, then cut each one into four pieces.

FOR THE CODIUM BUTTER

Roughly chop the codium. Mix the butter and codium in a Thermomix® at 205°F (95°C) for a few minutes on low speed. Increase to high speed until the butter is creamy, then reduce the speed and let cook for 25 minutes.
Strain through a chinois and let clarify in the refrigerator. Once the butter has clarified, separate the fat from the whey and reserve both.

FOR THE OYSTER FOAM

7 oz. (200 g) oysters
1 3/4 oz. (50 g) codium whey (reserved from codium butter)
1/4 tsp. (0.5 g) xanthan gum
Scant 1/4 cup (1 3/4 oz./50 g) codium butter

FOR THE CODIUM OIL

3 1/2 oz. (100 g) codium (seaweed)
3/8 cup (90 ml) grapeseed oil
2 tsp. mild olive oil

FOR THE CODIUM TEMPURA

3/4 cup + 1 tbsp. (3 1/2 oz./100 g) pastry (soft) flour
1 egg yolk
7/8 cup (200 ml) sparkling water
1 oz. (25 g) codium (seaweed)
Unrefined sea salt
Sunflower oil, for frying

FOR THE LIME GEL

1 cup (250 ml) lime juice
3 1/2 tsp. (1/4 oz./7 g) agar-agar powder

FOR THE PUFFED RICE

1/4 cup (1 3/4 oz./50 g) white rice
1 cup + 1 tbsp. (250 ml) water
2 cups + 2 tbsp. (500 ml) sunflower oil
Salt

FOR THE WILTED SORREL

1 3/4 oz. (50 g) fresh sorrel
1 tsp. codium oil

FOR THE OYSTER FOAM

Prepare the oysters as above and cook on a charcoal grill. Once they are well smoked, blend them with the reserved codium whey and the xanthan gum. Gradually add the codium butter until emulsified. Strain through a fine-mesh sieve. Pour into a small siphon fitted with a gas cartridge and keep warm.

FOR THE CODIUM OIL

Roughly chop the codium. Mix with the two oils in a Thermomix® at 205°F (95°C) for a few minutes on low speed. Increase to high speed until creamy, then reduce the speed and let cook for 10 minutes.
Strain through a chinois and let clarify in the refrigerator. Separate the fat from the liquid and store the oil in a pipette in the fridge.

FOR THE CODIUM TEMPURA

In a bowl, mix the flour with the egg yolk, then gradually mix in the sparkling water. Season with salt.
Separate the codium into sprigs, then dip them into this tempura batter. Deep fry at 355°F (180°C). Set aside.

FOR THE LIME GEL

In a saucepan, boil the lime juice with the agar-agar for 2 minutes, while whisking continuously. Let cool, then blend. Transfer to a pipette and set aside in the refrigerator.

FOR THE PUFFED RICE

Wash the rice three times in cold water. Put the rice and water into a saucepan, season with a little salt, and cook for 10 minutes. Strain and place in a desiccator at 131°F (55°C) for 8 hours.
Fry the rice in the sunflower oil at 355°F (180°C/gas 4). Drain and store in an airtight container.

FOR THE WILTED SORREL

Wash and dry the fresh sorrel. Remove the central stem from each leaf. Tear the leaves into tiny pieces with your hands. In a very hot skillet (frying pan), sauté the sorrel in the codium oil for a few seconds.

TO SERVE

Make a bed of wilted sorrel in each oyster shell. Place a grilled oyster on top. Add a few grains of puffed rice and five dots of lime gel.
Cover everything with the oyster foam. Finish with the codium tempura and a few drops of codium oil.

LAMB **MILLEFEUILLE**

SERVES 4

FOR THE DRIED LEAVES
8 chard leaves
8 green cabbage leaves
8 sea lettuce leaves
4 nori sheets
Olive oil

FOR THE FRESH LEAVES
8 mustard leaves
8 iceberg lettuce leaves
8 red orache leaves

FOR THE LAMB
1 leg of lamb
1 carrot
1 onion
1 celery stalk
1/3 cup + 2 tbsp. (3 1/2 oz./100 g) butter
3 qt. + 7/8 cup (3 L) lamb stock
Olive oil

FOR THE CANDIED KOMBU
5/8 cup (150 ml) water
5/8 cup (150 ml) soy sauce
Scant 1/4 cup (50 ml) mirin
1/2 cup (3 1/2 oz./100 g) superfine (caster) sugar
2 kombu sheets

FOR THE SAUCE
7/8 cup (200 ml) lamb cooking juices
1 oz. (30 g) candied kombu

FOR THE SEAWEED MAYONNAISE
3 egg yolks
Pinch of salt
A few drops of lemon juice
1 1/4 cups (300 ml) sunflower oil
3/4 oz. (20 g) fisherman's salad (mix of dried seaweed flakes)

FOR THE DRIED LEAVES

In a skillet (frying pan) over high heat, brown the leaves in a drizzle of olive oil. Dry them in a desiccator at 122°F (50°C) for at least 6 hours.

FOR THE FRESH LEAVES

Wash the leaves thoroughly then drain them. Set aside in the refrigerator.

FOR THE LAMB

Heat a drizzle of olive oil in a skillet. Brown the leg of lamb on all sides. Remove from the pan and set aside. Dice the vegetables and, in the same skillet, fry them in the butter.

Place the browned lamb and vegetables in a Dutch oven (casserole dish). Cover with the lamb stock, then cook for 2 hours in a wood-fired oven. The lamb should be very tender.

Let the lamb cool in the stock. Once the meat is cold, cut it into 3/4 in. (2 cm) slices. Remove the vegetables from the stock and reduce.

FOR THE CANDIED KOMBU

In a saucepan, stir together the water, soy sauce, mirin, and sugar. Bring to a boil, then reduce the heat to the lowest setting. Immerse the kombu in this marinade and cook over low heat for 20 minutes. Remove from the heat and let cool in the liquid.

Cut the kombu into julienne strips and set it aside in the cooking liquid.

FOR THE SAUCE

In a saucepan, stir the candied kombu into the lamb cooking juices. Heat over low heat and keep warm until serving.

FOR THE SEAWEED MAYONNAISE

Place the egg yolks in a bowl with the salt and lemon juice. Using an immersion blender, blend while gradually adding the sunflower oil. Then, add the fisherman's salad and blend again.

Transfer this mayonnaise to a pastry (piping) bag. Set aside in the refrigerator.

TO SERVE

In a dish, stack the dried and fresh leaves, alternating them and using the seaweed mayonnaise to stick them together. Place a piece of lamb between two iceberg lettuce leaves. Continue to assemble the millefeuille using the dried and fresh leaves. Finish with a large cabbage leaf, then place a spoonful of sauce to the left of it.

LEAVES —— FALL P. 98

MATE AND WHITE CHOCOLATE

SERVES 4

FOR THE GANACHE
1/2 cup (120 ml) whipping cream
4 tsp. (1/4 oz./8 g) ground yerba mate
1/5 silver gelatin leaf (0.5 g)
5 oz. (150 g) white chocolate

FOR THE MATE DULCE DE LECHE
2 cups (480 ml) whole milk
3 tbsp. (3/4 oz./20 g) ground yerba mate
1/2 cup + 1 tbsp. (4 1/4 oz./120 g) superfine (caster) sugar

FOR THE MATE ICE CREAM
3 1/2 tbsp. (1 1/2 oz./40 g) superfine (caster) sugar
2/3 cup (3 3/4 oz./106 g) dextrose
1/4 cup (1 oz./30 g) low-fat (semi-skimmed) powdered milk
3 tbsp. (3/4 oz./20 g) ground yerba mate
1 3/4 cups (420 ml) whole milk
1/2 cup (120 ml) whipping cream
1 tbsp. (3/4 oz./20 g) inverted sugar syrup

FOR THE MATE MERINGUE
1/3 cup + 1 1/2 tbsp. (100 ml) water
4 1/2 tbsp. (1 oz./30 g) ground yerba mate
2 tbsp. (1/3 oz./10 g) powdered egg white
1/2 cup (3 1/2 oz./100 g) superfine (caster) sugar
1/2 cup (3 1/2 oz./100 g) isomalt

FOR THE MILK CRISPS
1 1/2 tbsp. superfine (caster) sugar
1 1/4 tbsp. powdered milk
Scant 1 tsp. (1.4 g) gellan gum
1/2 cup (120 ml) whole milk

FOR THE GANACHE

In a saucepan, boil the cream then stir in the mate. Let infuse in the refrigerator overnight. Strain through a Superbag®.
Soak the gelatin in a little iced water. Break the chocolate into pieces and place in a bowl. Boil the mate cream then pour it over the chocolate. Add the drained gelatin, stir well, then set aside in the refrigerator.

FOR THE MATE DULCE DE LECHE

In a saucepan, boil the milk, then stir in the mate and let infuse for 24 hours in the refrigerator.
Strain through a Superbag® into a saucepan, then stir in the sugar and cook over very low heat for at least 4 hours. Once the mixture has reduced, pour it into a stainless-steel container and set aside in the refrigerator.

FOR THE MATE ICE CREAM

In a saucepan, mix all the ingredients and heat to 175°F (80°C). Chill to 39°F (4°C), then set aside in the refrigerator overnight.
The next day, strain through a Superbag®, then churn in an ice cream maker.

FOR THE MATE MERINGUE

In a saucepan, heat the water to 175°F (80°C) then stir in 1 1/2 tablespoons (1/3 oz./10 g) of the mate. Let infuse for 5 minutes then strain through a Superbag®. Let cool. Stir the powdered egg white into the mate infusion then pour into the bowl of a stand mixer. Whisk gently.
In another saucepan, mix the sugar and isomalt and heat to 244°F (118°C). Then, pour over the egg white and infusion mix. Continue to whisk until the meringue forms stiff peaks.
Spread the mixture onto a silicone baking mat in a thin (2 mm) layer, then sprinkle with the remaining 3 tablespoons (3/4 oz./20 g) ground mate. Dry in the oven at 200°F (90°C) for 3 hours.
Once the meringue is very dry, break it into pieces about 3/4 in. (2 cm) long, and store in airtight containers.

FOR THE MILK CRISPS

Place all the ingredients in a saucepan and bring to a boil. Pour the mixture into a stainless-steel container. Let cool in the refrigerator.
Once the mixture is hard, blend until very smooth. Spread out on a silicone baking mat in a thin (2 mm) layer. Let dry in a desiccator at 131°F (55°C) for 3 hours. Before serving, burn it with a kitchen blowtorch.

(RECIPE CONTINUES OVERLEAF)

FOR THE KOMBUCHA GELATIN
1/3 cup + 1 1/2 tbsp. (100 ml) water
1 1/2 tbsp. (1/3 oz./10 g) ground yerba mate
1/3 cup + 1 1/2 tbsp. (100 ml) mate kombucha
1 1/2 tsp. (2.8 g) agar-agar powder

FOR THE CRYSTALLIZED LEAVES
Scant 1 tbsp. (1/3 oz./10 g) superfine (caster) sugar
2 tsp. water
1 3/4 oz. (50 g) egg whites
4 lemon balm leaves
4 mint leaves
4 marigold leaves
Ground yerba mate

FOR THE MATE CHOCOLATE
3 1/2 oz. (100 g) white chocolate
Ground yerba mate

FOR THE KOMBUCHA GELATIN

In a saucepan, heat the water to 175°F (80°C) then stir in the ground yerba mate. Let infuse for 5 minutes then strain through a Superbag®. Add the kombucha and agar-agar and boil for 2 minutes while whisking.

Using a piston funnel, spread the mixture onto cold marble in as thin a layer as possible. Once it has set, cut out leaves from the gelatin using a leaf-shaped cookie (pastry) cutter (about 3/4 in./2 cm long).

FOR THE CRYSTALLIZED LEAVES

In a saucepan, dissolve the sugar in the water and heat to make a syrup. In a bowl, mix the egg white with the syrup. Dip each leaf into this mixture then sprinkle with mate. Place in a desiccator at 131°F (55°C) and dry overnight. Store in an airtight container.

FOR THE MATE CHOCOLATE

Temper the white chocolate then spread it onto acetate paper. Before it hardens, sprinkle it with yerba mate. Store in the refrigerator, then cut into irregular-shaped pieces.

TO SERVE

Pipe a small ring of ganache in the center of a dish. Fill the hole with some of the mate dulce de leche. Top with a quenelle of mate ice cream.
Then, arrange the milk crisps, mate white chocolate, and pieces of the mate meringue around the edge. Finish with the crystallized leaves and the kombucha gelatin.

OXALIS AND CRAB

SERVES 4

FOR THE CRABMEAT
1 large crab, weighing 3 1/4 lb. (1.5 kg)
1 1/3 cups (10 1/2 oz./300 g) butter
Zest of 1 orange

FOR THE CRAB JELLY
8 1/4 oz. (230 g) crab shell
1 1/2 cups (350 ml) water
1 1/2 silver gelatin leaves (4 g)
4 tsp. (1/4 oz./8 g) agar-agar powder

FOR THE SORREL CREAM
1 silver gelatin leaf (2 g)
3 1/2 oz. (100 g) fresh sorrel
Scant 1/4 cup (50 ml) whipping cream

TO SERVE
1 lime
Green heart-shaped oxalis leaves
Citronnette (see page 252)
Unrefined sea salt

FOR THE CRABMEAT

Using a knife, pierce a hole in the center of the crab's head. Make a funnel from a piece of foil and place it in the hole. Place the crab in a stainless-steel container. Add the butter and orange zest. Cook in a combi oven at 165°F (75°C) with 20% humidity for 25 minutes. Every 7 minutes, using a ladle, pour the hot butter into the hole to ensure that the crabmeat is well cooked.
Remove from the oven and let cool at room temperature. Crack the shell and remove all the crabmeat. Set aside in the refrigerator.

FOR THE CRAB JELLY

In a large stand mixer, crush the crab shell to obtain a creamy paste. If the crab shell is too big or too hard, crush it with a hammer before mixing. Pour this mixture into a saucepan, add the cold water and bring to a boil over low heat. Once the paste rises to the surface, strain through a chinois and then through a Superbag®. Soak the gelatin leaves in a little cold water. Weigh out 5/8 cup (150 ml) of this consommé, then, in a saucepan, bring to a boil a scant 1/4 cup (50 ml) of it with the agar-agar. Boil for 2 minutes, while whisking. Drain the gelatin, dissolve it in the hot liquid, then pour this over the remaining 3/8 cup (100 ml) of cold consommé. Using a piston funnel, spread the mixture onto cold marble. Let cool, then cut into 4 in. (10 cm) disks using a 4 in. (10 cm) diameter cookie (pastry) cutter. Set aside between sheets of guitar paper.

FOR THE SORREL CREAM

Soak the gelatin leaf in a little cold water. Remove the stems from the sorrel then place the leaves in a blender. Boil the cream and pour it over the sorrel. Blend until smooth. Strain through a chinois then add the drained gelatin. Once the gelatin has dissolved, let cool in the refrigerator. Transfer to a pastry (piping) bag.

TO SERVE

Supreme the lime then dice the flesh. Stick the oxalis leaves onto the crab jelly circles. In a bowl, season the crabmeat with the citronnette and unrefined sea salt. Place a dot of sorrel cream in the center of a plate. Add three lime cubes around it. Place the crabmeat on top, then carefully cover everything with the crab jelly and oxalis veil.

RED BELGIAN ENDIVE
AND BLEU DU QUEYRAS SAUCE

SERVES 4

FOR THE GINGER REDUCTION
1 oz. (30 g) fresh ginger
1/3 cup + 1 1/2 tbsp. (100 ml) water
1/2 cup (3 1/2 oz./100 g) superfine (caster) sugar
2 tbsp. beet (beetroot) juice
2 tbsp. rice vinegar
1/5 oz. (5 g) dried hibiscus flowers

FOR THE RED BELGIAN ENDIVES
2 red Belgian endives
1 1/2 tbsp. (3/4 oz./20 g) butter
The ginger reduction
Red berry vinegar
Fleur de sel

FOR THE BLEU DU QUEYRAS SAUCE
7 oz. (200 g) Bleu du Queyras cheese without the rind
7/8 cup (200 ml) whipping cream

FOR THE HIBISCUS GEL
Scant 2 cups (450 ml) water
1/4 cup (1 3/4 oz./50 g) superfine (caster) sugar
Zest of 1 orange
Zest of 1 lemon
1 tsp. (5 g) cracked black pepper
1 clove
1/2 vanilla bean (pod)
1 3/4 oz. (50 g) dried hibiscus flowers
4 tsp. (1/4 oz./8 g) agar-agar powder

TO SERVE
8 Grenoble walnuts
12 raw red Belgian endive tips
Red shiso sprouts

FOR THE GINGER REDUCTION

Peel the ginger, then cut it into fine strips using a mandoline. In a saucepan, heat the water with the sugar. Add the beet (beetroot) juice, rice vinegar, and dried hibiscus flowers. Add the ginger and let cook over low heat for 1 hour, until transparent. Strain through a chinois, then reduce again until the sauce has the consistency of caramel.

FOR THE RED BELGIAN ENDIVES

Cut the endives in half lengthwise. In a skillet (frying pan), heat the butter, then brown the cut sides of the endives. Add a little of the ginger reduction and glaze. Then, deglaze with a dash of red berry vinegar. Turn the endives over and season with a few grains of fleur de sel. Set aside.

FOR THE BLEU DU QUEYRAS SAUCE

Dice the cheese. In a saucepan, heat the cream, then stir in the cheese. Let it melt over low heat. Strain through a chinois and keep warm.

FOR THE HIBISCUS GEL

In a saucepan, stir together the water, sugar, citrus zests, spices, and hibiscus flowers. Heat to 175°F (80°C), then let infuse for 30 minutes. Strain through a chinois, pressing it down using a ladle. You will need 1 1/4 cups (300 ml) of the liquid. Add the agar-agar and boil for 2 minutes while whisking. Pour into a stainless-steel container and let cool. Once the gel has set, blend until smooth. Transfer to a pipette.

TO SERVE

Place a good quantity of the Bleu du Queyras sauce into a dish. Add half a Belgian endive, cut face upward.
Top with a few dots of hibiscus gel, some crushed walnuts, the raw endive tips, and the red shiso shoots.
To serve, add three drops of the ginger reduction to the sauce.

LEAVES —— WINTER P. 107

RADICCHIO RAVIOLI AND WILD BOAR CONSOMMÉ

SERVES 4

FOR THE WILD BOAR CONSOMMÉ
1 oz. (30 g) onion (1/4 cup diced)
1 oz. (30 g) carrot (1/4 cup diced)
2 garlic cloves
1 tsp. (5 g) juniper berries
1/2 tbsp. (5 g) black peppercorns
2 bay leaves
2 tsp. (1/3 oz./10 g) unrefined sea salt
2 1/2 tbsp. muscovado sugar
7/8 cup (200 ml) red wine
2 1/4 lb. (1 kg) wild boar
8 cups (2 L) water

FOR THE CANDIED CHESTNUTS
1 cup (3 1/2 oz./100 g) peeled chestnuts
Scant 1/4 cup (1 3/4 oz./50 g) butter
2 1/2 tbsp. (1 3/4 oz./50 g) acacia honey
2 tsp. (1/3 oz./10 g) unrefined sea salt

FOR THE RADICCHIO FILLING
1 lb. 2 oz. (500 g) 'Rosso di Treviso Tardivo' radicchio
Scant 1/4 cup (1 3/4 oz./50 g) butter
5 juniper berries
5 black peppercorns
1/2 cup (125 ml) red wine
3 1/2 oz. (100 g) raw foie gras
2 tsp. (1/3 oz./10 g) red miso

FOR THE BLACK RAVIOLI
1 cup (4 1/2 oz./125 g) pastry (soft) flour
Scant 1/4 cup (1 1/2 oz./40 g) semolina
4 egg yolks
1 tbsp. vegetable carbon
8 cups (2 L) water
Unrefined sea salt

TO SERVE
1 'Rosso di Treviso Tardivo' radicchio
Olive oil

FOR THE WILD BOAR CONSOMMÉ

Wash the vegetables and cut them into mirepoix. In a baking pan, stir together the vegetables, spices, sugar, and red wine. Cut the meat into pieces, then place them into this marinade. Let marinate in the refrigerator for 12 hours.
The next day, remove from the refrigerator and pour in enough water to cover. Lay a sheet of parchment (baking) paper over the top, in contact with the meat, then cover the pan with foil. Cook in a dry oven at 265°F (130°C/gas 1) for 12 hours. Once the meat is cooked, strain the cooking juices through a chinois lined with parchment (baking) paper to clarify.

FOR THE CANDIED CHESTNUTS

Mix all the ingredients in a sous-vide bag, then cook in a steam oven at 185°F (85°C) for 1 hour 30 minutes. Once the chestnuts are cooked, let cool, then cut into quarters. Store at room temperature.

FOR THE RADICCHIO FILLING

Using a mandoline, cut the radicchio into thin strips. In a large saucepan, melt the butter, then stir in the radicchio strips.
Tie the crushed juniper berries and crushed peppercorns into a little cheesecloth (muslin) bag and add to the saucepan. Pour in the red wine, then cook over low heat until the radicchio is tender, about 30 minutes.
Press the foie gras through a sieve to remove any lumps and veins. Let the radicchio cool, then chop it finely. You should have 1 lb. 2 oz. (500 g) of filling. Stir in the sieved foie gras and the red miso. Transfer the mixture to a pastry (piping) bag.

FOR THE BLACK RAVIOLI

In a stand mixer fitted with the paddle attachment, mix the flour, semolina, egg yolks, and vegetable carbon until you have a smooth dough. Let rest in the refrigerator for 1 hour.
On a work surface dusted with flour, roll the dough out to 1/16 in. (2 mm) thick. On the half of the dough nearest to you, place a little of the radicchio filling at 1 1/4 in. (3 cm) intervals. Brush the upper part of the dough with water, then fold it over to cover the filling. Press down on the dough to seal it around each portion of filling. Using a pastry wheel, cut the dough into 1 1/4 in. (3 cm) ravioli. Set aside on a baking sheet dusted with flour.
In a large saucepan, bring the water to a boil with a pinch of salt, then add the ravioli and cook for 5 minutes. Drain and serve hot.

TO SERVE

Cut the tips from the radicchio and set aside in iced water.
Place five black ravioli in a dish and add three quarters of candied chestnut and three radicchio tips. Serve the wild boar consommé very hot over the top and add a few drops of olive oil.

LEAVES —— WINTER P. 108

CHOCOLATE AND **ROSEMARY**

SERVES 4

FOR THE CHOCOLATE CREAM
1/2 silver gelatin leaf (1.4 g)
1/3 cup + 1 tbsp. (95 ml) whole milk
3/4 oz. (20 g) egg yolk
1 tbsp. (1/2 oz./13 g) muscovado sugar
2 1/4 oz. (60 g) bittersweet chocolate
1 tsp. (5 g) cocoa powder
4 tsp. (20 ml) olive oil

FOR THE CHARRED ROSEMARY ICE CREAM
1 oz./25 g fresh rosemary leaves
1 cup + 2 tbsp. (270 ml) whole milk
1/3 cup (80 ml) whipping cream
1/2 cup less 1 tbsp. (2 1/2 oz./70 g) dextrose
3 tbsp. (3/4 oz./20 g) low-fat (semi-skimmed) powdered milk
2 tbsp. (1 oz./25 g) superfine (caster) sugar
2 tsp. (1/2 oz./12 g) inverted sugar syrup

FOR THE CACAO NIB COOKIES
1/4 cup (1 3/4 oz./50 g) superfine (caster) sugar
Scant 1/4 cup (1 3/4 oz./50 g) butter
1 tbsp. milk
2 tsp. (1/2 oz./15 g) glucose syrup
1/2 cup (2 1/4 oz./60 g) cacao nibs
Scant 1/2 cup (1 1/2 oz./40 g) ground almonds
Unrefined sea salt

FOR THE CHOCOLATE VEIL
1 egg
3/4 cup (5 oz./150 g) superfine (caster) sugar
1/3 cup + 1 1/2 tbsp. (100 ml) olive oil
1/4 tsp. (1 g) unrefined sea salt
1/2 cup (2 1/4 oz./65 g) pastry (soft) flour
1/4 cup (1 oz./30 g) cocoa powder
1/4 tsp. (1 g) baking soda (bicarbonate of soda)
1/4 tsp. (1 g) baking powder
1/3 cup (75 ml) orange juice
1/2 cup (120 ml) milk
Butter spray

FOR THE CHOCOLATE CREAM

Soak the gelatin in a little iced water. Bring the milk to a boil in a saucepan. In a bowl, whisk the egg yolk and sugar together, then pour over the hot milk, while continuing to whisk. Pour the mixture back into the saucepan and heat over low heat, stirring continuously with a spatula.
Heat this cream to 180°F (82°C), then stir in the drained gelatin. Break the chocolate into pieces and place in heatproof bowl with the cocoa powder. Pour the hot cream over the chocolate and cocoa and whisk. Cool to 86°F (30°C), then emulsify with the olive oil. Cover the surface with plastic wrap (cling film) and let cool.
Once the cream is cold, transfer it to a pastry (piping) bag fitted with a round tip (nozzle).

FOR THE CHARRED ROSEMARY ICE CREAM

Wash and dry the rosemary, then char it using a kitchen blowtorch. Set aside.
Place all the remaining ingredients in a saucepan, stir together, then heat to 185°F (85°C). Add the charred rosemary.
Let stand overnight in the refrigerator. Strain through a chinois, then through a Superbag®. Churn in an ice cream maker.

FOR THE CACAO NIB COOKIES

Preheat the oven to 320°F (160°C/gas 3). Put the sugar, butter, milk, and glucose syrup in a saucepan and bring to a boil. Add the cacao nibs and ground almonds. Stir well and season with a pinch of unrefined sea salt.
Roll out the cookie dough as thinly as possible between two sheets of parchment (baking) paper. Transfer to a baking sheet and bake in the oven for 10 minutes. Let cool, then cut into small pieces. Store in an airtight container.

FOR THE CHOCOLATE VEIL

In a stand mixer, beat the egg with the sugar. Gradually drizzle in the olive oil and mix to obtain an emulsion. Sift all the dry ingredients into another bowl. Add to the egg, sugar, and oil mixture, alternating with the orange juice and milk.
Line a stainless-steel baking pan with a silicone baking mat of the same size and spray with butter spray. Spread 7 oz. (200 g) of the chocolate mixture into the pan in an even layer. Cook in a steam oven at 250°F (120°C) for 30 minutes. Transfer to a dry oven at 285°F (140°C/gas 1) and cook for a further 3 minutes.
Remove from the oven and let cool. Using a cookie (pastry) cutter, cut out 6 in. (15 cm) diameter circles. Store the disks in an airtight container separated with parchment (baking) paper to prevent them sticking to each other.

LEAVES —— WINTER P. 110

FOR THE CHOCOLATE POWDER
3 eggs
3 1/2 tbsp. (1 1/2 oz./40 g) superfine (caster) sugar
1/3 cup (1 1/2 oz./40 g) all-purpose (plain) flour
Scant 1 tbsp. (1/3 oz./10 g) baking powder
1 1/2 tbsp. (1/3 oz./10 g) cocoa powder

FOR THE ROSEMARY POWDER
3 1/2 oz. (100 g) fresh rosemary

TO SERVE
Olive oil

FOR THE CHOCOLATE POWDER

Preheat the oven to 350°F (175°C/gas 4). Mix all the ingredients together in a Thermomix®. Pour the mixture into a baking pan and bake in the oven for 40 minutes, then place in a desiccator at 140°F (60°C) for 24 hours. Blend to a fine powder.

FOR THE ROSEMARY POWDER

In a saucepan, blanch the rosemary leaves three times, using fresh water each time. Place in a desiccator at 140°F (60°C) for 12 hours, then blend to a fine powder.

TO SERVE

Place some chocolate cream in the center of a dish. Make a hole in the center and pour in a little olive oil.
Place three pieces of cacao nib cookie around the edge and top with a scoop of the charred rosemary ice cream. Cover with the chocolate veil and sprinkle with the chocolate and rosemary powders.

ROSE TUILES AND SMOKED MACKEREL

SERVES 4

FOR THE ROSE TUILES

1 1/4 cups (5 oz./150 g) pastry (soft) flour
2 tbsp. (1 oz./25 g) cold butter
5 tsp. (25 ml) sunflower oil,
plus extra for sticking the powder
2 1/4 oz. (60 g) egg whites
Scant 1 tsp. (4 g) salt
Dried rose powder

FOR THE SMOKED MACKEREL CREAM

1 3/4 oz. (50 g) smoked mackerel
(trimmings, skin and head)
1/3 cup + 1 1/2 tbsp. (100 ml)
whipping cream (1)
1/2 silver gelatin leaf (1 g)
Scant 1/4 cup (50 ml) whipping cream (2)

FOR THE ROSE PICKLES

1 whole rose
1/2 cup (125 ml) cider vinegar
1/2 cup (125 ml) red berry vinegar
1/3 cup (75 ml) water
1/4 cup (1 3/4 oz./50 g) superfine
(caster) sugar

TO SERVE

4 cubes of smoked mackerel
(1/2 x 1/2 in./1 x 1 cm)

FOR THE ROSE TUILES

Preheat the oven to 350°F (175°C/gas 4). In a stand mixer fitted with the hook attachment, beat the flour, butter, and sunflower oil. Once the mixture is smooth, add the egg whites and salt. Continue mixing until the dough comes away from the sides of the bowl. Be careful not to overmix it: the dough should not get hot. Roll the dough out to 1/8 in. (3 mm) thick. Using a cookie (pastry) cutter, cut out 1 1/4 in. (3 cm) diameter circles. Bake in the oven for 40 minutes.
When the tuiles are cooked, brush the edges with a little oil and stick the rose power to them.

FOR THE SMOKED MACKEREL CREAM

Cut the mackerel into little pieces and mix with the cream (1). Cook sous vide in a steam oven at 150°F (65°C) for 2 hours. Strain, pressing well to obtain as much flavor as possible.
Soak the gelatin in a little water. Measure 1/3 cup + 1 1/2 tbsp. (100 ml) of the infused cream and add the drained gelatin and the cream (2). Whisk, then transfer to a pastry (piping) bag and refrigerate.

FOR THE ROSE PICKLES

Remove the petals from the rose and arrange them in a dish. Place the cider vinegar, red berry vinegar, water, and sugar in a saucepan and bring to a boil. Pour the hot pickle mixture over the rose petals and let cool at room temperature. Set aside in the refrigerator.

TO SERVE

Pipe a dot of the smoked mackerel cream in the center of each rose tuile. Add a cube of smoked mackerel. Cover with the rose pickles.

FLOWERS —— SPRING P. 116

CHRYSANTHEMUM DOME, FLAKED CRAB, AND SPRING FLOWERS

MAKES ABOUT 12 DOMES

FOR THE MERINGUE DOME
1/4 cup (65 ml) orange juice
1/4 tsp. (0.5 g) xanthan gum
1 tbsp. (1/2 oz./12 g) superfine (caster) sugar
2 3/4 oz. (75 g) fresh egg whites
1 tbsp. (5 g) powdered egg white
2 tbsp. (1/2 oz./15 g) confectioners' (icing) sugar

FOR THE SHELLFISH CREAM
1 carrot
1/2 celery stalk
1/2 leek white
1/2 onion
3 1/2 oz. (100 g) shellfish heads
1 tbsp. butter
1 tsp. (4 g) tomato paste (purée)
1 green cardamom pod
1 star anise
Zest of 1 untreated lime
1 tbsp. white wine
1 tsp. Cognac

FOR THE SHELLFISH SAUCE ROYALE
1/3 cup + 1 1/2 tbsp. (100 ml) cream
1/3 cup + 1 1/2 tbsp. (100 ml) shellfish cream
2 tsp. (1/3 oz./10 g) yellow miso
1 tsp. (4 g) tomato paste (purée)
1 oz. (30 g) egg
3/4 oz. (20 g) egg yolk
1 pinch unrefined sea salt

FOR THE CHRYSANTHEMUM GEL
7/8 cup (200 ml) orange juice
1/4 oz. (8 g) dried 'Snowflake' chrysanthemum
4 tsp. (1/4 oz./8 g) agar-agar powder

FOR THE CRAB MIX
1 scant cup (4 1/4 oz./120 g) crabmeat
2 tbsp. (5 g) snipped chives
1 1/2 tbsp. (1/3 oz./10 g) finely chopped shallot
2 tbsp. crème fraîche
1 pinch unrefined sea salt
A few drops of lemon juice
Drizzle of olive oil

TO SERVE
Mixed flowers (cosmos, marigold, elderflower, sage, pansy, carrot)

FOR THE MERINGUE DOME

In a bowl, stir together the orange juice, xanthan gum, and superfine (caster) sugar. In the bowl of a mixer, whip the fresh and powdered egg whites until the latter has completely dissolved. Increase the speed to maximum and whip the egg whites to soft peak stage, then gradually add the orange juice mixture. Sift in the confectioners' (icing) sugar and, using a rubber spatula, stir it in.

Transfer to a pastry (piping) bag fitted with a plain tip (nozzle) then pipe the mixture into a 3 in. (8 cm) diameter silicone half-sphere molds. Using a spoon, empty the center of each dome. Smooth the edges with the spatula. Dry in the oven at 200°F (90°C) for 3 hours.

Unmold and set the meringue domes aside in a desiccator.

FOR THE SHELLFISH CREAM

Dice the carrot, celery, leek, and onion. Brown the shellfish heads in the butter. Remove from the pan and fry the diced vegetables until tender. Return the shellfish heads to the pan and stir in the tomato paste (purée), spices, and lime zest. Deglaze with the white wine and Cognac, and reduce until all the liquid has evaporated. Add water to cover, and cook over low heat for 40 minutes. Blend in a Thermomix®, then strain through a chinois, pressing down well.

FOR THE SHELLFISH SAUCE ROYALE

Using an immersion blender, blend all the ingredients, then strain through a chinois. Pour the mixture into an ovenproof pan to 2/3 in. (15 mm) thick. Cook, covered, in a steam oven at 185°F (85°C) for 30 minutes. Check for doneness and let cool. The sauce should have the consistency of panna cotta.

FOR THE CHRYSANTHEMUM GEL

In a small saucepan, bring the orange juice to a boil. Add the flowers then let infuse for 10 minutes. Strain and reserve the liquid. Add the agar-agar and boil for 2 minutes while whisking.

Pour into a container and set aside in the refrigerator. When it is cold, blend until smooth. Store it in a pipette in the refrigerator.

FOR THE CRAB MIX

Flake the crabmeat. In a bowl, mix the crabmeat with all the other ingredients. Set aside in the refrigerator.

TO SERVE

Place half a tablespoon of the shellfish sauce Royale on a plate. Place the crab mix on top and give it some volume.

Stick the flowers onto the meringue dome using the chrysanthemum gel. Place the dome over the crab.

PETIT POIS AND **ELDERFLOWER** RAGOUT

SERVES 4

FOR THE PETIT POIS RAGOUT

2 tbsp. (1/2 oz./15 g) finely chopped shallot
1 oz. (10 g) cod tripe
2 tbsp. (1 oz./30 g) butter
4 tsp. (20 ml) elderflower vinegar
2 1/4 cups (11 1/4 oz./320 g) fresh petit pois
2 tbsp. (5 g) snipped chives
Unrefined sea salt

TO SERVE

Elderflowers

FOR THE PETIT POIS RAGOUT

In a skillet (frying pan), sweat the shallot. Finely dice the cod tripe and add to the skillet with the butter and the elderflower vinegar. Stir well to create an emulsion. Season with salt.

At the last moment, stir in the petit pois and the chives. Let cool before serving.

TO SERVE

Place some of the petit pois ragout in a small dish and top with the elderflowers.

NASTURTIUM FLOWER
AND CUCUMBER

SERVES 4

FOR THE CUCUMBER JUICE
1 lb. 2 oz. (500 g) cucumber
2 tbsp. (1 oz./30 g) superfine (caster) sugar

FOR THE CUCUMBER BALLS
1 cucumber
The cucumber juice

FOR THE NASTURTIUM OIL
1 1/4 cups (300 ml) sunflower oil
3 1/2 oz. (100 g) nasturtium leaves

FOR THE NASTURTIUM FLOWER ICE CREAM
Scant 2 cups (450 ml) whole milk
1/3 cup + 1 tbsp. (90 ml) whipping cream
2 tsp. (1/2 oz./15 g) inverted sugar syrup
1/3 cup + 2 1/2 tbsp. (2 1/2 oz./70 g) dextrose
2 tbsp. (1 oz./30 g) superfine (caster) sugar
3 tbsp. (3/4 oz./21 g) low-fat (semi-skimmed) powdered milk
1 tsp. (3 g) carob flour
2 1/2 oz. (70 g) nasturtium flower petals

FOR THE NASTURTIUM FLOWER PURÉE
The nasturtium flower pulp reserved from the ice cream

FOR THE NASTURTIUM LEAF POWDER
10 1/2 oz. (300 g) nasturtium leaves

TO SERVE
4 whole nasturtium flowers

FOR THE CUCUMBER JUICE

Blend the whole cucumbers then strain through a Superbag®. In a saucepan, dissolve the sugar in a little of the cucumber juice, then add the remaining juice. Stir, then refrigerate.

FOR THE CUCUMBER BALLS

Peel the cucumber and make balls using a small melon baller. Place the balls in the cucumber juice, then place in a sous-vide machine to absorb some of the liquid. Set the balls aside in their remaining juice in the refrigerator.

FOR THE NASTURTIUM OIL

In a Thermomix®, blend the oil with the nasturtium leaves at 45°F (70°C) for 10 minutes. Pour into a container and refrigerate for at least 12 hours.
The following day, strain through a Superbag® without squeezing it. Transfer the oil to a pipette and set aside.

FOR THE NASTURTIUM FLOWER ICE CREAM

In a saucepan, heat the milk, cream, and inverted sugar syrup at 104°F (40°C). Then, add the dextrose, sugar, powdered milk, and carob flour and cook, stirring continuously, until the mixture reaches 185°F (85°C). Blend the hot cream with the nasturtium flowers. Refrigerate for 24 hours.
Strain through a Superbag®, reserving the petal pulp. Churn the strained mixture in an ice cream maker.

FOR THE NASTURTIUM FLOWER PURÉE

Place the reserved nasturtium petal pulp in the bowl of a Pacojet® and freeze. Churn twice in the Pacojet®, then transfer to a pastry (piping) bag.

FOR THE NASTURTIUM LEAF POWDER

In a desiccator, dry the nasturtium leaves at 150°F (65°C) for 12–16 hours. Once they are completely dry, blend them and reserve the powder in a sealed container.

TO SERVE

Place seven cucumber balls and three dots of nasturtium purée in each dish. Add a few drops of nasturtium oil and the nasturtium leaf powder. Place a quenelle of nasturtium flower ice cream on top of the cucumber. Decorate with a whole nasturtium flower.

FLOWERS —— SPRING P. 122

COSMOS VEIL AND VEAL TARTARE

SERVES 4

FOR THE VEAL TARTARE
7 oz. (200 g) veal
1 shallot, finely chopped
2 tbsp. (5 g) snipped chives
1 oz. (30 g) mostarda di Cremona, finely diced
Olive oil
Red berry vinegar
Unrefined sea salt

FOR THE VEAL GELATIN
1 silver gelatin leaf (3 g)
3/4 cup + 1 tbsp. (190 ml) clarified veal stock
1 1/2 tsp. (3 g) agar-agar powder

FOR THE RASPBERRY GEL
1 cup (8 3/4 oz./250 g) raspberry pulp
Scant 2 tsp. (3.5 g) agar-agar powder

FOR THE RASPBERRY VINEGAR
1 2/3 cups (7 oz./200 g) fresh raspberries
1 1/2 tbsp. (1/3 oz./10 g) finely chopped shallot
1/8 oz. (3 g) peeled fresh ginger
1/2 tsp. (3 g) unrefined sea salt
Zest and juice of 1 untreated lime
1/3 cup + 1 1/2 tbsp. (100 ml) extra virgin olive oil
1 tbsp. red berry vinegar

TO SERVE
80 cosmos petals of different colors

FOR THE VEAL TARTARE

Finely chop the meat, as for a tartare. Mix with the shallot, chives, and mostarda di Cremona. Season with a drizzle of olive oil, vinegar, and salt. Set aside in the refrigerator.

FOR THE VEAL GELATIN

Soak the gelatin in a little water. Boil the veal stock with the agar-agar for 2 minutes, whisking continuously. Remove from the heat and add the drained gelatin. Stir well.
Using a piston funnel, spread the gelatin onto cold marble. Let cool, then cut into 4 in. (10 cm) diameter disks. Set aside in the refrigerator.

FOR THE RASPBERRY GEL

In a saucepan, mix the raspberry pulp and agar-agar, boil for 2 minutes, whisking continuously. Pour the mixture into a container and let cool in the refrigerator. Once it has set, blend to obtain a smooth gel. Store in a container in the refrigerator.

FOR THE RASPBERRY VINEGAR

Place all the ingredients in a saucepan, heat gently, and let infuse for 30 minutes, then strain though a chinois, pressing down with a ladle. Set aside in the refrigerator.

TO SERVE

Stick the cosmos petals onto the veal gelatin disks like fish scales. Set aside.
In a dish, place the veal tartare as flat as possible in a 4 in. (10 cm) circle. Spread with a thin layer of the raspberry gel, then stick the flower-covered gelatin disk on top.
Finally, drizzle some raspberry vinegar around the edge.

FLOWERS —— SUMMER P. 126

SUNFLOWER RAVIOLI AND PARMESAN BOUILLON

SERVES 4

FOR THE RAVIOLI DOUGH
10 egg yolks
2 cups + 1 tbsp. (8 3/4 oz./250 g) pastry (soft) flour

FOR THE SUNFLOWER FILLING
3 1/2 oz. (100 g) sunflower heads
Olive oil
1 shallot, finely chopped
Scant 1/4 cup (3/4 oz./20 g) grated Parmesan
Unrefined sea salt

FOR THE EGG YOLK SAUCE
4 egg yolks
1/3 cup + 1 1/2 tbsp. (100 ml) olive oil
1 thyme sprig
3 garlic cloves
1 bay leaf
Salt

FOR THE PARMESAN BOUILLON
2 cups + 2 tbsp. (500 ml) water
3 1/2 oz. (100 g) Parmesan rind
1/3 oz. (10 g) kombu (dried kelp)
1 tsp. colatura di alici (Italian fermented anchovy sauce)
Unrefined sea salt

FOR THE CAVIAR DOME
1/4 cup (2 1/4 oz./60 g) Ossetra caviar
1 tsp. (5 g) sunflower pollen

TO SERVE
Sunflower petals
Unrefined sea salt

FOR THE RAVIOLI DOUGH

In a stand mixer fitted with the paddle attachment, beat the egg yolks with the flour. Incorporate the eggs well but do not overwork the dough. Let rest in the refrigerator, covered with a clean kitchen (tea) towel, for 30 minutes.

FOR THE SUNFLOWER FILLING

Clean the flowers by removing the petals, green parts and pollen. Reserve the petals and pollen.
Dice half the flower heads. In a very hot skillet (frying pan), fry them in a drizzle of olive oil. Set aside.
Cut the other half of the flowers into strips. In a saucepan, sweat the shallot in a drizzle of olive oil. Add the flower strips and cook for 10 minutes. Add a little water, then cover with parchment (baking) paper and cook for 20 minutes. Season with unrefined sea salt. Once tender, remove from the heat and blend in a Thermomix®. Mix with the cooked diced sunflowers. Add the grated Parmesan and transfer to a pastry (piping) bag. Set aside.

MAKING THE RAVIOLI

Roll the dough out to 1/16 in. (2 mm) thick. Using a 2 3/4 in. (7 cm) cookie (pastry) cutter, cut out disks. Pipe some filling onto half of the disks. Cover each filled disk with another disk of dough and press to seal the edges, brushing with a little water if necessary. Set aside on a baking sheet dusted with flour.

FOR THE EGG YOLK SAUCE

Place the egg yolks into a baking pan, pour over the olive oil, and add the thyme, garlic, and bay leaf. Cook in the oven at 140°F (60°C) for 40 minutes. Using an immersion blender, blend the egg yolks with a little of the cooking oil and some salt until you have a creamy sauce. Transfer to a pastry (piping) bag and set aside at room temperature.

FOR THE PARMESAN BOUILLON

In a saucepan, stir together the water, Parmesan rind, and kombu. Reduce by half over low heat. Strain then reduce again. Strain through paper towels to remove excess fat. Season with the colatura di alici and a little salt.

FOR THE CAVIAR DOME

On a sheet of parchment (baking) paper, form domes of caviar, each weighing 1/2 oz. (15 g), using a 3/4 in. (2 cm) melon baller. Insert the pollen between the grains of caviar. Set aside in the refrigerator.

TO SERVE

Cook the ravioli in salted boiling water for 3 minutes.
Place the cooked ravioli in the center of a dish. Cover with the egg yolk sauce and arrange the sunflower petals around the outside. Place the caviar dome in the center. Serve the hot Parmesan bouillon separately.

FLOWERS —— SUMMER P. 128

ZUCCHINI FLOWER
RAVIOLI AND CHICKEN CONSOMMÉ

SERVES 4

FOR THE CHICKEN CONSOMMÉ WITH THYME
4 1/2 lb. (2 kg) chicken carcasses
1 onion
1 carrot
1 celery stalk
1 tsp. black pepper
1 clove
2 thyme sprigs
1 bay leaf
3 1/4 qt. (3 L) water
Olive oil

TO CLARIFY THE CONSOMMÉ (FOR 4 1/4 CUPS/1 L)
1 oz. (30 g) onion (1/4 cup finely diced)
1 oz. (30 g) carrot (1/4 cup finely diced)
1/3 oz. (10 g) celery (2 tbsp. finely diced)
3 1/2 oz. (100 g) chicken breast
2 egg whites

FOR THE CHICKEN STUFFING
1 shallot
3 1/2 oz. (100 g) chicken breast
2 3/4 oz. (75 g) egg whites
1/3 cup (75 ml) whipping cream
4 tsp. (20 ml) Armagnac
Olive oil
Unrefined sea salt

FOR THE ZUCCHINI (COURGETTE) RAVIOLI
6–12 zucchini (courgette) flowers (depending on their size)
The chicken filling

FOR THE GARNISH
1 yellow zucchini (courgette)
1 green zucchini (courgette)
Scant 1/4 cup (50 ml) white balsamic vinegar

TO SERVE
Chickweed sprouts

FOR THE CHICKEN CONSOMMÉ WITH THYME

Preheat the oven to 355°F (180°C/gas 4). Brown the chicken carcasses in the oven for 30 minutes until golden brown. Cut the vegetables into mirepoix. In a skillet (frying pan), heat a drizzle of olive oil and brown the diced vegetables.
Place the browned chicken carcasses, vegetables, spices, 1 thyme sprig, and the bay leaf into a large pot. Cover with cold water. Bring to a boil and boil for 10 minutes, then lower the heat, cover, and cook gently for 48 hours. Strain through a chinois, then let chill and skim off the fat.
To clarify, wash the vegetables and cut them into mirepoix. Cut the chicken breast into little pieces. Blend the vegetables in a Thermomix®, add the chicken, blend again, then add the egg whites and blend until smooth.
Pour the cold stock into a large saucepan and heat gently. When it reaches 95–99°F (35–37°C), add the blended chicken and vegetables. Bring to a gentle boil, while stirring continuously. When the mixture begins to rise, stop stirring and let it cook until the consommé is clear and the meat totally cooked.
Strain it through a chinois lined with parchment (baking) paper. Before serving, add a thyme sprig to the consommé and let infuse.

FOR THE CHICKEN STUFFING

Finely chop the shallot then fry it in a pan with a drizzle of olive oil without browning. Let cool.
Blend the chicken breast with the egg whites, cream, and cooked shallot. Season with the Armagnac and unrefined sea salt. Ensure that you keep the temperature cold while blending. The mixture should be smooth and creamy. Strain through a fine-mesh sieve. Let cool then transfer to a pastry (piping) bag.

FOR THE ZUCCHINI (COURGETTE) RAVIOLI

Remove the stems from the flowers and cut each flower in half lengthwise. Arrange them in 3/4 in. (2 cm) diameter half-sphere silicone molds. Fill each mold with the chicken stuffing. Use the same zucchini flower to cover the filling. Freeze, then unmold. Set aside in the refrigerator.
Before serving, cook the ravioli in a steam oven at 210°F (100°C) for 5 minutes.

FOR THE GARNISH

Cut each zucchini in half. Slice one half into thin strips using a mandoline. With the other half, form balls using a small melon baller. Immerse the yellow balls in the white balsamic vinegar.

TO SERVE

Place three zucchini ravioli in a dish. Add the green and yellow zucchini balls and strips. Garnish with a few chickweed sprouts. Finally, pour the hot chicken consommé into the bottom of the dish.

FLOWERS —— SUMMER P. 130

POLLEN, HONEY, AND PROPOLIS

SERVES 4

FOR THE MEAD JELLY
4 gold gelatin leaves (8 g)
3/8 cup (90 ml) water
1 cup + 1 tbsp. (250 ml) mead

FOR THE FERMENTED HONEY ICE CREAM
1 3/4 cups (425 ml) milk
1/2 cup + 1 tbsp. (130 ml) whipping cream
1/2 cup + 3 tbsp. (3 3/4 oz./105 g) dextrose
3 tbsp. (1 1/4 oz./37 g) superfine (caster) sugar
1 1/2 tbsp. (1 oz./30 g) fermented honey
1/4 cup (1 oz./30 g) low-fat (semi-skimmed) powdered milk

FOR THE PROPOLIS CREAM
1 cup + 1 tbsp. (250 ml) whipping cream
2 tsp. (1/2 oz./12 g) propolis
1/2 cup (4 1/2 oz./125 g) mascarpone

FOR THE HONEY TUILES
1/3 cup + 1 1/2 tbsp. (1 3/4 oz./50 g) pastry (soft) flour
1/3 cup (1 1/2 oz./40 g) confectioners' (icing) sugar
1 oz. (25 g) egg white
2 3/4 tbsp. (1 1/2 oz./40 g) whipping cream
2 tsp. (1/2 oz./15 g) honey

FOR THE POLLEN GRANITA
Scant 2 cups (450 ml) water
2 tbsp. (1 oz./25 g) superfine (caster) sugar
5 tsp. (1 oz./25 g) pollen

FOR THE WAX STREUSEL
5 tsp. (25 g) food-grade wax (natural beeswax)
1/2 cup (3 1/2 oz./100 g) superfine (caster) sugar
1/3 cup (2 3/4 oz./75 g) butter
3/4 cup + 1 tbsp. (3 1/2 oz./100 g) all-purpose (plain) flour
1 cup + 1 tbsp. (3 1/2 oz./100 g) ground almonds
1/3 tsp. (2 g) salt

TO SERVE
1 beehive frame with honey
Royal jelly
Pollen grains

FOR THE MEAD JELLY

Soak the gelatin in a little water. In a saucepan, boil the water. Remove from the heat and dissolve the drained gelatin in the water. Add the mead, stir well, then pour into a container. Let set in the refrigerator.

FOR THE FERMENTED HONEY ICE CREAM

In a saucepan, mix all the ingredients and heat to 185°F (85°C). Chill to 39°F (4°C), then set aside in the refrigerator overnight. Churn in an ice cream maker.

FOR THE PROPOLIS CREAM

In a saucepan, heat half the cream with the propolis. Let cool. In a mixing bowl, mix the infused cream with the remaining cream and the mascarpone, then whip it using a hand-held electric mixer. Set aside in the refrigerator.

FOR THE HONEY TUILES

In a bowl, stir together the flour and sugar. Gradually pour in the egg white, cream, and honey. Mix well to prevent lumps and too much air.
Transfer the mixture to a silicone honeycomb mold. Cook in a fan oven at 302°F (150°C) for 6 minutes. Carefully unmold it while still hot, then cut into tuiles using a cookie (pastry) cutter.

FOR THE POLLEN GRANITA

Pour the water, sugar, and pollen into a saucepan and heat until the sugar has dissolved. Pour into a container and freeze. Using a fork, scrape the granita. Store it in the freezer.

FOR THE WAX STREUSEL

Preheat the oven to 315°F (155°C/gas 2). Temper the wax, then, in a stand mixer, cream it with the sugar and butter. Add the flour, ground almonds, and salt and mix well but without overworking the dough. Crumble onto a silicone baking mat and bake in the oven for 10–12 minutes. Mix briefly in a food processor then sieve. Store in a sealed container at room temperature.

TO SERVE

Arrange a few pieces of mead jelly in a bowl. Place a scoop of fermented honey ice cream on top. Add a little of the wax streusel, then cover with a large spoonful of the propolis whipped cream.
Cover with pollen granita. Finish by placing a honey tuile on top. Cut a piece of honeycomb from the frame and place it on the dessert, then drizzle some of the honey from the frame on top. Decorate with a little royal jelly and a few grains of pollen.

FLOWERS —— SUMMER P. 134

HIBISCUS AND BEET ROSE

SERVES 4

FOR THE BEET (BEETROOT)

4 1/2 lb. (2 kg) Guérande unrefined sea salt
7/8 cup (200 ml) water
1 crapaudine beet (beetroot)

FOR THE VEAL CARPACCIO

2 1/4 lb. (1 kg) lean veal meat
Soy sauce

FOR THE HIBISCUS GEL

Scant 2 cups (450 ml) water
1/4 cup (1 3/4 oz./50 g) superfine (caster) sugar
Zest of 1 untreated orange
Zest of 1 untreated lemon
1 tsp. cracked black pepper
1 clove
1/2 vanilla bean (pod)
1 3/4 oz. (50 g) dried hibiscus flowers
4 tsp. (1/4 oz./8 g) agar-agar powder

FOR THE BEET (BEETROOT) AND HIBISCUS VINAIGRETTE

1/3 cup + 1 1/2 tbsp. (100 ml) olive oil
1/3 cup + 1 1/2 tbsp. (100 ml) beet (beetroot) juice
Scant 1/4 cup (50 ml) hibiscus infusion (reserved from gel base)
Unrefined sea salt

FOR THE HIBISCUS POWDER

1 3/4 oz. (50 g) dried hibiscus flowers

FOR THE BEET (BEETROOT)

Preheat a dry oven to 350°F (180°C/gas 4). In a bowl, stir the salt into the water. Line an ovenproof dish with parchment (baking) paper, then spread with a fine layer of salt. Add the beet (beetroot) and cover it completely with the remaining salt. Bake the beet in the oven for about 3 hours. Check for doneness using a cooking probe. Remove from the oven and let rest for 30 minutes at room temperature. Remove the beet from its salt crust and peel.

Using a meat slicer, cut the beet into thin slices, then cut into disks using a 1 1/2 in. (4 cm) diameter cookie (pastry) cutter. Set aside in the refrigerator.

FOR THE VEAL CARPACCIO

Clean the meat and mold it into a shape as round as possible before freezing. Remove from the freezer and cut it into very fine slices using a meat slicer or mandoline. Season with soy sauce and set aside in the refrigerator.

FOR THE HIBISCUS GEL

In a saucepan, mix the water with the sugar, orange and lemon zests, spices, and hibiscus flowers. Heat to 175°F (80°C), then let infuse for 30 minutes. Strain through a chinois, pressing it down using a ladle. You will need 1 1/4 cups (300 ml) of the liquid. Reserve a scant 1/4 cup (50 ml) for the vinaigrette.

Place the remaining hibiscus infusion in a small saucepan with the agar-agar and boil for 2 minutes. Pour into a container and let cool. Once the gel has set, blend it until smooth. Transfer to a pipette and set aside in the refrigerator.

FOR THE BEET (BEETROOT) AND HIBISCUS VINAIGRETTE

Mix together all the ingredients to make a vinaigrette and set aside in a pipette.

FOR THE HIBISCUS POWDER

Blend the hibiscus flowers and set aside the resulting powder in an elasticated food cover or fine-mesh sieve.

TO SERVE

On a stainless-steel baking sheet, create roses by interspersing the beet slices with the veal carpaccio (use the hibiscus gel to help them stick together). Sprinkle the roses with the hibiscus powder.

Pour a little of the beet and hibiscus vinaigrette into a dish and place a rose on top.

FLOWERS —— FALL P. 136

LOBSTER AND **VANILLA**

SERVES 4

FOR THE CELERY ROOT (CELERIAC)
1 celery root (celeriac)

FOR THE VANILLA SKEWERS
4 vanilla beans (pods)

FOR THE LOBSTER
2 live Mediterranean lobsters, each weighing about 14 oz.–1 lb. 5 oz. (400–600 g)
3 1/4 qt. (3 L) water
4 tsp. (3/4 oz./20 g) clarified butter

FOR THE VANILLA SAUCE
1 shallot
1/3 cup + 1 1/2 tbsp. (100 ml) cider vinegar
1 3/4 sticks (7 oz./200 g) cold butter
Pulp of 1 vanilla bean (pod) (obtained from the skewers)
Salt

TO SERVE
5 fresh thyme sprigs
5 fresh marjoram sprigs
5 fresh rosemary sprigs
5 fresh oregano sprigs
5 fresh wormwood sprigs
5 fresh pine sprigs
Charcoal

FOR THE CELERY ROOT (CELERIAC)

Using a mandoline, cut the celery root (celeriac) into 3/4 in. (2 cm) slices. Grill on both sides over charcoal. Remove from the grill (barbecue) and, using a 1 1/2 in. (4 cm) flower-shaped cookie (pastry) cutter, cut out flowers then cut each flower in half.

FOR THE VANILLA SKEWERS

Split the vanilla beans (pods) lengthwise and scrape out the seeds. Set aside this pulp for making the vanilla sauce. Dry the beans in a desiccator until hard enough to serve as skewers.

FOR THE LOBSTER

Tie the live lobsters by the tail, or pierce through the back with a wooden spike. Boil the lobsters in the water for 4 minutes then set aside. Remove the head and shell. Cut the flesh into medallions following the lines of the lobster.
Place three lobster medallions and three pieces of celery root on each vanilla skewer, alternating them. Brush with the clarified butter and reheat gently in the salamander before serving.

FOR THE VANILLA SAUCE

Peel and finely chop the shallot. Place the shallot and vinegar in a small saucepan and reduce by half over low heat.
Strain and reserve the liquid. Use it to make a *beurre monté* in a saucepan over low heat. Dice the cold butter and add to the pan, whisking continuously. Add the vanilla pulp. Season with salt.

TO SERVE

Line the bottom of a cast-iron or copper pan with foil, leaving a hole in the middle. Fill around the hole with the herbs, adding volume. Place the lobster skewers on top of the herbs and cover the pan. Before serving, place the hot charcoal in the hole to create a smoker. Present at the table, remove the lid, arrange a skewer on each plate, and pour over the vanilla sauce.

FLOWERS —— FALL P. 138

ARTICHOKE TART

SERVES 12 (MAKES A 12 IN./30 CM TART)

FOR THE ARTICHOKE PURÉE
11 lb. (5 kg) Breton artichokes
Ascorbic acid
Olive oil
1 thyme sprig
1 bay leaf
Unrefined sea salt

FOR THE ARTICHOKE STRIPS
25 spiny artichokes
3 Macau artichokes
Ascorbic acid
Unrefined sea salt

FOR THE PUFF PASTRY
8 1/3 cups (2 1/4 lb./1 kg) pastry (soft) flour
2 cups + 1 tbsp. (500 ml) water
3/4 cup + 2 tbsp. (7 oz./200 g) softened butter
4 tsp. (3/4 oz./20 g) salt
1 lb. 10 oz. (750 g) sheet butter
(12 x 15 in./30 x 40 cm)

FOR THE FILLING
3 1/4 oz. (90 g) Comté cheese 36 months
1 oz. (30 g) black truffle

FOR THE SAUCE PÉRIGORD
Scant 1/4 cup (1 oz./30 g) finely chopped shallot
2 tsp. Madeira wine
2 tsp. ruby port
1 tsp. sherry vinegar
1 cup + 1 tbsp. (250 ml) veal stock
1/2 oz. (15 g) black truffle
Olive oil

FOR THE CITRONNETTE
1 1/4 cups (300 ml) mild oil
1/2 cup (120 ml) lemon juice
1 1/2 tbsp. (1 oz./25 g) yellow mustard
Unrefined sea salt

FOR THE ARTICHOKE PURÉE

Prepare the artichokes: turn them, scoop out the insides, and thinly slice the hearts. Set aside in a bowl of water with a little ascorbic acid added.
Drain the artichokes well. Add a drizzle of olive oil to a Dutch oven (casserole dish) and cook the artichokes, without browning them, with the thyme, bay leaf, and salt until tender. Blend to obtain a very smooth purée. Cool in a bain-marie.

FOR THE ARTICHOKE STRIPS

Clean the artichokes and cut into strips. Set aside in a bowl of water with a little ascorbic acid added to prevent oxidization. Cook them for 45 seconds in boiling water with a little ascorbic acid and salt. Strain and set aside in the refrigerator.

FOR THE PUFF PASTRY

Knead the flour with the water, softened butter, and salt to obtain a smooth dough. Let rest for 20–30 minutes in the refrigerator.
Preheat the oven to 340°F (170°C/gas 4). Roll out the dough into a 20 x 24 in. (50 x 60 cm) rectangle and place the very cold sheet of butter in the center. Next, fold into three, then roll out again, turn and repeat six times.
Roll out to a thickness of 1/8 in. (3 mm), cut out a 9 1/2 in. (24 cm) diameter circle and line an 8 in. (20 cm) diameter pie plate (tart tin). Cover with foil and add weights (rice or lentils). Chill before blind baking in the oven for 15 minutes. Serrate the edge using scissors.

FOR THE FILLING

Using a mandoline, cut the Comté into thin slices and spread them over the puff pastry. Finely chop the truffle.

FOR THE SAUCE PÉRIGORD

In a saucepan, sweat the shallot in a drizzle of olive oil. Deglaze with the Madeira, port, and vinegar. Reduce to half over low heat, then pour in the veal stock. Cook until the sauce has a velvety texture. Chop the truffle and stir into the sauce.

FOR THE CITRONNETTE

Blend all the ingredients to obtain a stable dressing. Set aside in the refrigerator.

TO SERVE

Preheat the oven to 355°F (180°C/gas 4). Using a spatula, spread the artichoke purée over the strips of Comté in the pie crust (pastry case). Scatter over the chopped black truffle. Arrange the artichoke strips on top to form a flower and cook in the oven for 8–10 minutes.
Once the tart is cooked, cut into slices and serve with the sauce Périgord on one side and the citronnette on the other.

FLOWERS —— FALL P. 142

YUCCA AND GRAPEFRUIT

SERVES 4

FOR THE STRACCIATELLA CREAM
3 1/2 oz. (100 g) Stracciatella di bufala
Scant 1/4 cup (50 ml) whipping cream
Scant 1/4 cup (1 oz./25 g) confectioners' (icing) sugar

FOR THE GRAPEFRUIT SORBET
1 1/2 cups (10 1/2 oz./100 g) superfine (caster) sugar
1 1/2 cups (350 ml) water
1/4 cup + 1 tbsp. (1 2/3 oz./46 g) dextrose
1 tsp. (4 g) carob flour
1 1/4 cups (300 ml) grapefruit juice
Scant 1/4 cup (50 ml) lemon juice

FOR THE ALMOND FOAM
4 silver gelatin leaves
2 cups + 2 tbsp. (500 ml) almond milk
3 tbsp. (1 1/4 oz./35 g) superfine (caster) sugar
2 tbsp. water
2 tsp. (1/3 oz./10 g) orgeat syrup

FOR THE GARNISHES
12 almonds
40 yucca flower petals
1 pink grapefruit

FOR THE STRACCIATELLA CREAM

In a bowl, mix the stracciatella with the cream and confectioners' (icing) sugar. Set aside in the refrigerator.

FOR THE GRAPEFRUIT SORBET

In a saucepan, mix the sugar, water, dextrose, and carob flour. Heat to 185°F (85°C), then let cool to 39°F (4°C). Once the mixture is cold, stir in the grapefruit juice and lemon juice. Let stand overnight in the refrigerator, then churn in an ice-cream maker. Store at 5°F (-15°C).

FOR THE ALMOND FOAM

Soak the gelatin in a little iced water until soft. In a saucepan, heat half the almond milk with the sugar and water. Squeeze dry the gelatin and stir it into the hot milk. Once the gelatin has dissolved, stir in the remaining cold almond milk and the orgeat syrup. Let cool in the refrigerator until the gelatin has begun to set. Blend using an immersion blender then pour into a small siphon fitted with one gas canister. Set aside in the refrigerator.

FOR THE GARNISHES

Preheat the oven to 340°F (170°C/gas 4), then toast the almonds for 10 minutes. Let cool and set aside.
Remove the petals from the yucca and set aside in the refrigerator.
Supreme the grapefruit and dice the flesh. Set aside.

TO SERVE

Place a tablespoon of the stracciatella cream in a dish. Arrange three toasted almonds and place three cubes of grapefruit in the center.
Add a quenelle of grapefruit sorbet. Cover everything with the almond foam then arrange the yucca petals around the outside.

FLOWERS —— FALL P. 144

BORAGE FLOWERS AND RAZOR CLAMS

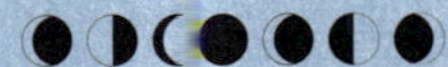

SERVES 4

FOR THE SEAFOOD FLAN

FIRST STEP: STOCK BASE

1/2 oz. (15 g) kombu kelp
2 cups + 2 tbsp. (500 ml) water
1 oz. (25 g) katsuobushi (bonito flakes)

SECOND STEP: FLAN

1 1/4 cups (300 ml) stock base
1/4 cup (60 ml) white miso
5 oz. (150 g) eggs

THIRD STEP: FINISH

1/2 silver gelatin leaf (1.25 g)
1/3 cup + 1 1/2 tbsp. (100 ml) stock base

FOR THE RAZOR CLAMS

2 1/4 lb. (1 kg) medium-size razor clams
3 1/4 qt. (3 L) water
1/3 cup (90 g) unrefined sea salt (for disgorging the clams)
5/8 cup (150 ml) stock base
2 tbsp. sesame oil
Scant 1/4 cup (50 ml) rice vinegar
2 tsp. lemon juice
1 tsp. (6 g) unrefined sea salt

TO SERVE

Borage flowers

FOR THE SEAFOOD FLAN

In a saucepan, simmer the kombu in water at 140°F (60°C) for about 2 hours. Remove the kombu, raise the temperature and add the katsuobushi for 30 seconds. Strain through a chinois, then let cool.

In a stand mixer or blender, mix the cold stock base, the white miso, and the eggs. Place 2 tablespoons of this mixture into each of four glasses. Place the glasses in a dish and cover with a damp clean kitchen (tea) towel. Cook in a steam oven at 185°F (85°C) for 30 minutes. Let cool.

Soak the gelatin leaf in a little cold water. In a saucepan, heat the stock base and add the drained gelatin. When the gelatin has dissolved, cover each flan with a tablespoon of this mixture. Let cool in the refrigerator.

FOR THE RAZOR CLAMS

Disgorge the razor clams in the water with the salt.

To make the marinade, in a bowl, stir together the stock base, sesame oil, rice vinegar, lemon juice, and salt.

Place the razor clams in a perforated pan and cook them in a steam oven at 210°F (100°C) for 4 minutes. Cool immediately in iced water.

Clean the razor clams and place them in the marinade for 30 minutes. Then, slice them diagonally into pieces about 1/8 in. (3 mm) thick.

TO SERVE

Remove the seafood flans from the refrigerator. Drain the razor clams and use them to cover half of a flan, standing them upright and overlapping them. Cover the other half with the borage flowers.

FLOWERS —— WINTER P. 148

OSMANTHUS, LANGOUSTINE, AND GREEN APPLE

SERVES 4

— FIRST DISH

FOR THE OSMANTHUS GEL
1 cup + 1 tbsp. (250 ml) water
2 tbsp. superfine (caster) sugar
1/5 oz. (5 g) dried osmanthus flowers
Scant 2 tsp. (3.5 g) agar-agar powder
5 tsp. (25 ml) lemon juice

FOR THE GREEN APPLE AND OSMANTHUS JELLY
4 Granny Smith apples
4 silver gelatin leaves (9 g)
4 tsp. (1/4 oz./8 g) agar-agar powder
1 tsp. dried osmanthus flowers

FOR THE LANGOUSTINES
4 langoustines

FOR THE APPLE VINAIGRETTE
1/3 cup + 1 1/2 tbsp. (100 ml) Granny Smith apple juice
Scant 1/4 cup (50 ml) olive oil
Scant 1/4 cup (50 ml) cider vinegar
Unrefined sea salt

TO SERVE
1 3/4 oz. (50 g) Granny Smith apple, cored and diced into (1/2 in./1 cm cubes)
1/3 oz. (10 g) preserved lemon peel strips
Unrefined sea salt

—— FIRST DISH

FOR THE OSMANTHUS GEL

Heat the water to 175°F (80°C), pour in the sugar and the osmanthus flowers. Let infuse for 5 minutes. Strain, pour into a small saucepan. Add the agar-agar and the lemon juice and boil for 2 minutes. Let cool, then blend. Transfer to a pipette and set aside in the refrigerator.

FOR THE GREEN APPLE AND OSMANTHUS JELLY

Using a juicer, recover the juice from the apples. Pour 1 1/4 cups (285 ml) of this juice into a saucepan and bring to a boil to clarify it, then let cool. Soak the gelatin leaves in iced water to hydrate.
Stir the agar-agar into the apple juice and boil for 2 minutes, whisking continuously. Remove from the heat and add the drained gelatin. Stir well.
Using a piston funnel, spread the gelatin onto a flat surface. Scatter over the osmanthus flowers. Once the gelatin is cold, cut out flowers using a shaped cookie (pastry) cutter. Set the flowers aside in the refrigerator separated with guitar paper.

FOR THE LANGOUSTINES

Remove the langoustine heads and set aside for the second dish. Blanch the langoustines for 30 seconds then place in iced water. Shell the langoustines and cut each one into five pieces.

FOR THE APPLE VINAIGRETTE

Mix together all the ingredients to make a vinaigrette and set aside in a pipette.

TO SERVE

In a dish, arrange the pieces of langoustine and season with the apple vinaigrette, the green apple cubes, and the preserved lemon strips. Add a few dots of osmanthus gel. Cover everything with the green apple and osmanthus jelly.

(RECIPE CONTINUES OVERLEAF)

— SECOND DISH

FOR THE LANGOUSTINE HEADS
The reserved langoustine heads
1 1/2 oz. (40 g) cooked langoustine
1 tsp. (3 g) finely chopped shallot
Scant 1 tbsp. (2 g) snipped chives
1/8 oz. (3 g) dried osmanthus flowers
Zest and juice of 1 untreated lime
Unrefined sea salt

FOR THE OSMANTHUS EMULSION
1/5 oz. (5 g) dried osmanthus flowers
1 cup + 1 tbsp. (250 ml) water
1 3/4 sticks (7 oz./200 g) cold butter, diced
1 tsp. lime juice
Unrefined sea salt

— THIRD DISH

FOR THE LANGOUSTINES
4 langoustines
Olive oil
Fleur de sel

FOR THE OSMANTHUS HOLLANDAISE
3 egg yolks
2 tsp. lemon juice
2 tsp. osmanthus-infused water
Scant 1/4 cup (1 3/4 oz./50 g) clarified butter
Unrefined sea salt

—— SECOND DISH

FOR THE LANGOUSTINE HEADS

Clean the heads so you can see inside the shells. Dice the cooked langoustine. In a bowl, season with the chopped shallot, snipped chives, osmanthus flowers, lime zest and juice, and unrefined sea salt. Stir together then fill the langoustine heads with this mixture.

FOR THE OSMANTHUS EMULSION

Infuse the osmanthus in the water at 175°F (80°C) for 5 minutes. Strain. Mix with the cold diced butter. Season with the lime juice and some salt. Use an immersion blender to create an emulsion.

TO SERVE

Place a langoustine head in a dish with the osmanthus flowers. Pour some osmanthus emulsion on top.

—— THIRD DISH

FOR THE LANGOUSTINES

Remove the langoustine heads. Blanch the langoustines for 30 seconds then place in iced water. Shell the langoustines and dry well.
In a hot skillet (frying pan) with a drizzle of olive oil, brown the langoustines on both sides. Season with a few grains of fleur de sel.

FOR THE OSMANTHUS HOLLANDAISE

In a skillet (frying pan), combine the egg yolks, lemon juice, infused water, and a pinch of unrefined sea salt. Heat gently while whisking vigorously to stir in air until the eggs are cooked.
Remove from the heat and gradually stir in the clarified butter. Add some infused water if needed. It should be liquid. Taste and season with unrefined sea salt. Pour into a small siphon fitted with a gas cartridge. Keep it warm.

TO SERVE

Serve the hot grilled langoustines with the osmanthus hollandaise to the side.

SAFFRON AND MUSSELS

SERVES 4

FOR THE YELLOW BEET (BEETROOT)
1 yellow beet (beetroot)

FOR THE MUSSELS
2 1/4 lb. (1 kg) mussels
1 garlic clove
1 cup + 1 tbsp. (250 ml) white wine
1/3 cup (1/3 oz./10 g) curly parsley
Olive oil

FOR THE SAFFRON SAUCE
1 cup + 1 tbsp. (250 ml) mussel cooking juices
20 saffron threads
Pinch of saffron powder
1 stick less 1 tbsp. (3 1/2 oz./100 g)
cold butter, diced
Unrefined sea salt
A few drops of lemon juice

TO SERVE
1 lime
1 raw yellow beet (beetroot)
20 Malabar spinach flowers
Olive oil
Fleur de sel

FOR THE YELLOW BEET (BEETROOT)

Clean the beet (beetroot) and wrap it in foil. Cook in the oven at 355°F (180°C/gas 4) for 1 hour 30 minutes. Remove the foil and peel the beet. Cut into irregular triangles.

FOR THE MUSSELS

Clean the mussels. In a skillet (frying pan), heat a little olive oil and add the crushed garlic clove. Tip in the mussels. When they begin to open, add the white wine and parsley. Let cook for 5 minutes then remove from the heat. Strain, reserving the cooking juices for making the sauce.
Let the mussels cool, then shell them. Remove the beards from the inside. Set aside in the refrigerator in a little of the cooking juice.

FOR THE SAFFRON SAUCE

Heat the mussel cooking juices with the saffron threads and powder. Add the cold diced butter and mix using an immersion blender. Season with salt. Strain through a chinois. Add a few drops of lemon juice before serving.

TO SERVE

Supreme the lime then dice the flesh. Peel the beet. Using a mandoline, cut the yellow beet into very thin slices, then, using a 1/2 in. (1 cm) cookie (pastry) cutter, cut out disks. Set aside in iced water. To serve, dry the beet disks and season them with olive oil and fleur de sel.
In a small skillet (frying pan), heat a ladleful of the saffron sauce with the mussels and cooked beet triangles.
Arrange some cubes of lime in a dish. Top with the beet and mussel ragout. Finish with the beet disks and five Malabar spinach flowers.

FLOWERS —— WINTER P. 154

VIOLET AND UNPASTEURIZED GOAT MILK

SERVES 10

FOR THE VIOLET ICE CREAM

1 cup + 1 tbsp. (260 ml) unpasteurized goat milk
3/8 cup (90 ml) whipping cream
2 tsp. (1/2 oz./15 g) inverted sugar syrup
1/3 cup + 2 1/2 tbsp. (2 1/2 oz./70 g) dextrose
2 tbsp. (1 oz./25 g) superfine (caster) sugar
3 tbsp. (3/4 oz./21 g) nonfat (skimmed) powdered milk
1 1/3 tsp. (3 g) carob flour
2 1/2 oz. (70 g) fresh violet petals

FOR THE MILK SAUCE

1 silver gelatin leaf
1/2 cup + 1 tbsp. (140 ml) unpasteurized goat milk
1/4 cup (60 ml) whipping cream
1/3 cup (1 1/4 oz./36 g) powdered milk
1 tbsp. (1/2 oz./12 g) superfine (caster) sugar

FOR THE CRISPY VIOLET MILK SKIN

1 1/4 cups (300 ml) unpasteurized goat milk
3 tbsp. (1 1/4 oz./36 g) superfine (caster) sugar
3 tbsp. (3/4 oz./23 g) powdered milk
2 scant tsp. (3.5 g) gellan gum
Fresh violets

FOR THE WHITE CHOCOLATE AND VIOLET GANACHE

1 cup (225 ml) whipping cream (1)
3 1/2 tsp. (1 oz./25 g) glucose syrup
3 1/2 tsp. (1 oz./25 g) inverted sugar syrup
10 3/4 oz. (305 g) white chocolate
2 cups (450 ml) whipping cream (2)
Violet essential oil

FOR THE VIOLET JUICE

1 cup + 1 tbsp. (250 ml) water
1/3 cup + 1 1/2 tbsp. (100 ml) violet syrup
1 1/4 oz. (35 g) dried butterfly pea flowers
1/2 tsp. citric acid
1/2 tsp. (1 g) xanthan gum

FOR THE VIOLET ICE CREAM

In a saucepan, heat the goat milk, cream, and inverted sugar syrup to 104°F (40°C). Then, add the dextrose, sugar, powdered milk, and carob flour, and cook, stirring continuously, until the mixture reaches 185°F (85°C).
Blend this hot base with the violet petals. Let infuse in the refrigerator for 24 hours, then strain through a Superbag®. Churn in an ice cream maker.

FOR THE MILK SAUCE

Soak the gelatin in a little water. In a saucepan, boil the goat milk with the cream, powdered milk, and sugar. Remove from the heat and add the drained gelatin. Stir in well, then let cool in the refrigerator.

FOR THE CRISPY VIOLET MILK SKIN

In a saucepan, stir together the goat milk, sugar, powdered milk, and gellan gum, then bring to a boil and boil for 2 minutes. Mix well using a whisk. Pour the mixture into a container and let cool in the refrigerator.
Once it is hard, blend to a smooth purée. Spread in a thin layer on a silicone baking mat. Scatter violet petals and whole flowers over the surface. Place in a desiccator overnight then store in a dry place.

FOR THE WHITE CHOCOLATE AND VIOLET GANACHE

In a saucepan, boil the cream (1), glucose syrup, and inverted sugar syrup. Place the white chocolate in a bowl and pour over the hot cream and syrup and melt to form a ganache. Stir in the cold cream (2). Let rest in the refrigerator for at least 3 hours.
Using a hand-held electric mixer, gently whisk the ganache, adding a few drops of violet essential oil.

FOR THE VIOLET JUICE

In a saucepan, heat the water and the violet syrup. Add the butterfly pea flowers and let infuse for 10 minutes until the liquid is brightly colored. Strain through a Superbag®, then add the citric acid and whisk. When the mixture is cold, mix in the xanthan gum to give it texture.

FLOWERS —— WINTER P. 156

FOR THE VIOLET OPALINE
10 1/2 oz. (300 g) fondant
1/2 cup + 1 tbsp. (7 oz./200 g) glucose syrup
1 1/3 oz. (38 g) Nougasec (Louis François®)
Fresh and dried violets

FOR THE VIOLET OPALINE

Preheat the oven to 340°F (170°C/gas 4). Place the fondant, glucose syrup, and Nougasec in a saucepan. Heat to 295°F (145°C) without browning it. Pour it onto a silicone baking mat. Let cool, then blend.

Spread half the mixture in a thin layer on a lightly greased and wiped silicone baking mat. Place in the oven to melt for 2–4 minutes. Repeat to make another opaline sheet. Scatter the fresh and dried violets over one of the sheets. Cover with the second opaline sheet, then place back in the oven for 3 minutes so that the two sheets fuse, trapping the violets. Remove from the oven, let cool, then store in a dry place.

TO SERVE

In a dish, place a dot of the whipped white chocolate and violet ganache on the right. Pour the milk sauce around the edge.

Top with a quenelle of violet ice cream, then cover with pieces of the violet opaline, alternating them with pieces of the crispy violet milk skin.

Finish with a little violet juice on the side.

FLOWERS —— WINTER P. 156

BABY FAVA BEAN TARTLET AND PISTACHIO

SERVES 4

FOR THE TARTLET SHELLS (CASES)

1 2/3 cups (7 oz./200 g) pastry (soft) flour
2 tbsp. (1 oz./30 g) softened butter
2 tbsp. sunflower oil
2 3/4 oz. (80 g) egg whites
Scant 1 tsp. (4 g) salt

FOR THE BABY FAVA (BROAD) BEAN STRIPS

2 cups + 2 tbsp. (1 lb. 2 oz./500 g) baby fava (broad) beans

FOR THE GOAT CHEESE FILLING

1 oz. (30 g) baby fava (broad) bean trimmings
2 1/4 cups (8 3/4 oz./250 g) fresh goat cheese
Scant 1/4 cup (50 ml) whipping cream
Unrefined sea salt
Voatsiperifery (Madagascar wild) pepper

FOR THE BABY FAVA (BROAD) BEAN AND PISTACHIO CONDIMENT

1 3/4 oz. (50 g) baby fava (broad) bean trimmings
1/3 cup (1 3/4 oz./50 g) pistachios, toasted
4 tsp. lemon juice
2 tsp. olive oil
Unrefined sea salt

TO SERVE

Thyme flowers

FOR THE TARTLET SHELLS (CASES)

Mix the flour, softened butter, and sunflower oil in a mixer fitted with the hook attachment. When the dough begins to come together, add the egg whites and salt. Continue mixing until the dough comes away from the sides of the bowl. Be careful not to overmix it: the dough should not get hot. Chill in the refrigerator for at least 30 minutes.

Preheat the oven to 340°F (170°C/gas 4). Roll out the dough to 1/8 in. (3 mm) thick. Using a cookie (pastry) cutter, cut out 3/4 in. (2 cm) diameter circles. Press into the 3/4 in. (2 cm) diameter holes of a pie pan (tartlet tin). Press down using another pie pan. Trim off any excess dough using a small knife. Bake in the oven for 6 minutes.

Remove from the oven, let cool, then carefully remove the tartlet shells (cases) from the molds. Rub the edge with an emery cloth or a Microplane® to obtain a smooth edge.

FOR THE BABY FAVA (BROAD) BEAN STRIPS

Peel the baby fava (broad) beans. Using a knife, cut each bean lengthwise into 1/8 in. (3 mm) thick slices. Place on a baking sheet lined with parchment (baking) paper. Reserve the trimmings.

FOR THE GOAT CHEESE FILLING

Finely chop the fava bean trimmings.

In a small bowl, stir the goat cheese together with the cream. Season with salt and pepper, then stir in the chopped fava bean trimmings. Pour the mixture into a pastry (piping) bag and set aside in the refrigerator.

FOR THE BABY FAVA BEAN (BROAD) AND PISTACHIO CONDIMENT

Finely chop the fava bean trimmings and the pistachios. Season with the lemon juice, olive oil, and salt.

TO SERVE

Place a dot of the goat cheese filling in the bottom of the tartlet shell. Arrange the baby fava bean strips around the edge, like petals. Cover the center with the baby fava bean and pistachio condiment. Sprinkle the thyme flowers on top.

FRUITS —— SPRING P. 162

CAESAR'S **MUSHROOM** TARTARE

SERVES 4

FOR THE PARMESAN CREAM

3 eggs
1/2 cup (1 3/4 oz./50 g) grated Parmesan
2 tbsp. (1 oz./25 g) cold butter
4 tsp. (20 ml) whipping cream
Unrefined sea salt

FOR THE MUSHROOM DUXELLES

8 3/4 oz. (250 g) Caesar's mushrooms (*Amanita caesarea*)
2 tsp. (1/3 oz./10 g) butter
2 tbsp. (1/2 oz./15 g) finely chopped shallot
Leaves of 1 thyme sprig
Unrefined sea salt

TO SERVE

2 hard Caesar's mushrooms
Fleur de sel

FOR THE PARMESAN CREAM

Place the eggs, Parmesan, and butter in a Thermomix® and cook at 185°F (85°C) for 5 minutes. When the eggs are cooked, add the cream and a little salt and mix again for a few minutes without heating to obtain a very smooth cream.

FOR THE MUSHROOM DUXELLES

Clean the mushrooms. Separate into harder and softer ones. Finely dice the softer ones, reserving two harder ones for presentation.
In a sauté pan, melt the butter then sweat the shallot with the thyme leaves. Add the chopped mushrooms and sauté for 5 minutes. Season with unrefined sea salt.

TO SERVE

Place a tablespoon of mushroom duxelles in a dish. Add five dots of the Parmesan cream around the edge. Cover everything with a carpaccio of the hard Caesar's mushrooms, made using a truffle shaver. Season with a few grains of fleur de sel.

FRUITS —— SPRING P. 164

RED AND WHITE **STRAWBERRIES** AND FOIE GRAS

SERVES 4

FOR THE FOIE GRAS
2 foie gras escalopes

FOR THE STRAWBERRY CONDIMENT
3 1/2 oz. (100 g) red strawberries
1 3/4 oz. (50 g) green (underripe) strawberries
2 tsp. sherry vinegar
Unrefined sea salt

FOR THE STRAWBERRY TUILE
12 1/4 oz. (350 g) red strawberries
2 1/2 tbsp. (2/3 oz./19 g) confectioners' (icing) sugar
3/4 tbsp. (1/4 oz./7 g) cornstarch (cornflour)
2 tsp. (6 g) xanthan gum

FOR THE DUCK CONSOMMÉ
3 duck carcasses
1/2 carrot
1/2 onion
1/4 celery stalk
3 1/4 qt. (3 L) water

FOR CLARIFYING THE BOUILLON
1/4 carrot
1/4 onion
1/4 celery stalk
1/3 cup + 1 1/2 tbsp. (100 ml) lean duck or chicken
2 egg whites
4 1/4 cups (1 L) duck consommé
Salt

TO SERVE
2 white (heirloom) strawberries
4 green (underripe) strawberries
2 red strawberries

FOR THE FOIE GRAS

Cook the cold foie gras escalopes in a griddle pan over low heat for 3 minutes on each side, so the grill marks are visible. Let rest for 5 minutes before slicing diagonally into 1/2 in. (1 cm) thick slices.

FOR THE STRAWBERRY CONDIMENT

Wash the strawberries and dry them well. Cook half the red strawberries on the grill. Once they are well cooked, transfer to a bowl and crush them using a fork. Finely dice the remaining red strawberries and all the green ones. Stir the diced and crushed strawberries together and season with the vinegar and some salt.

FOR THE STRAWBERRY TUILE

Wash the strawberries then blend them in a Thermomix®. Add the confectioners' (icing) sugar, cornstarch (cornflour), and xanthan gum and blend to a smooth purée. Sieve the mixture, then pour into a saucepan and heat to 175°F (80°C). Spread the mixture out on a silicone baking mat in a very thin (2 mm) layer. Let dry overnight in a desiccator.

FOR THE DUCK CONSOMMÉ

Preheat the oven to 355°F (180°C/gas 4). Place the duck carcasses in a baking pan and roast them in the oven for 40 minutes. They should be golden brown on all sides.
Finely dice the carrot, onion, and celery, then brown them in a skillet (frying pan). In a large saucepan, mix the cooked vegetables with the roast duck carcasses. Cover with the cold water. Bring to a boil, boil for 5 minutes, then reduce the heat and simmer for at least 12 hours.
Strain the stock and set aside in the refrigerator. For each quart (liter) of stock, clarify as follows.

FOR CLARIFYING THE BOUILLON

Dice the carrot, onion, and celery. In a food processor, mix the lean duck or chicken and the egg whites, then add the chopped vegetables and mix until smooth.
Add this paste to the cold consommé and cook over low heat without boiling. The egg white and meat will rise to the surface and solidify, leaving a clear bouillon. Gradually make a hole in the center of this solidified surface using a ladle. Strain the bouillon through a chinois lined with paper towels. Season to taste.

TO SERVE

Cut both the white strawberries and two of the green ones into thin slices, about 1/8 in. (3 mm) thick. Cut the red and remaining green strawberries into quarters. Set aside.
Place a teaspoon of the strawberry condiment in a dish. Top with a slice of foie gras. Arrange the green and red strawberry quarters to one side.
Cover everything with the sliced green and white strawberries alternating with pieces of the strawberry tuile. Pour the duck consommé around the edge.

FRUITS —— SPRING P. 168

TAGGIASCA OLIVE AND LEMON

SERVES 4

FOR THE LEMON BRUNOISE
1 Menton lemon

FOR THE LEMON CREAM
1/2 silver gelatin leaf (1.25 g)
1/2 cup (125 ml) lemon juice
3 eggs
3 tbsp. (1 1/4 oz./35 g) superfine (caster) sugar
3 1/2 oz. (100 g) white chocolate
2 tsp. (1/3 oz./10 g) cocoa butter

FOR THE BLACK OLIVE CONFIT
1 3/4 oz. (50 g) Taggiasca black olives
1/3 cup + 1 1/2 tbsp. (100 ml) water
2/3 cup (4 3/4 oz./135 g) superfine (caster) sugar

FOR THE CARAMELIZED BLACK OLIVES
3/4 oz. (20 g) Taggiasca black olives
1/4 cup (1 3/4 oz./50 g) superfine (caster) sugar
2 tsp. grapeseed oil

FOR THE BLACK OLIVE VEIL
3/4 cup (175 ml) water
3 1/2 tbsp. (2 3/4 oz./75 g) syrup from the olive confit
2 1/2 tbsp. (1 oz./30 g) superfine (caster) sugar
2 tsp. (4 g) agar-agar powder
1 3/4 tsp. (5 g) vegetable carbon

FOR THE NORI AND OLIVE CRISTALLINE
2 1/4 tbsp. (1 3/4 oz./50 g) syrup from the olive confit
1 3/4 tsp. (5 g) vegetable carbon
4 nori sheets

FOR THE LEMON BRUNOISE

Supreme the lemon, then finely chop the flesh.

FOR THE LEMON CREAM

Soak the gelatin in a little water. In a saucepan, boil the lemon juice. In a bowl, beat the eggs with the sugar. Pour over the hot lemon juice then pour the mixture back into the pan. Stir and simmer until it reaches 185°F (85°C). Add the drained gelatin and stir in. Break up the chocolate and place in another bowl with the cocoa butter. Pour over the egg and sugar mixture and mix well, then set aside in the refrigerator.

FOR THE BLACK OLIVE CONFIT

Pit the olives then blanch them twice. Make a syrup with the water and sugar, then add the olives and cook over low heat for about 30 minutes.

FOR THE CARAMELIZED BLACK OLIVES

Pit and slice the olives, then let dry overnight in a desiccator. When they are dry, heat a skillet (frying pan) over high heat, pour in the sugar (which should caramelize immediately), then straight away add the olives and sauté them. Stir in the oil and set aside.

FOR THE BLACK OLIVE VEIL

Place all the ingredients in a saucepan and bring to a boil. Immediately spread it out very thinly (1 mm) on a marble surface. Let cool for 10 minutes, then cut into 4 in. (10 cm) disks using a round cookie (pastry) cutter.

FOR THE NORI AND OLIVE CRISTALLINE

Mix the olive confit syrup with the vegetable carbon, then soak the nori sheets in this mixture until softened. Drain and cut out a 2 in. (5 cm) diameter disk, then place it flat in a desiccator and leave for 36 hours.

(RECIPE CONTINUES OVERLEAF)

FOR THE TAPENADE ICE CREAM

2 silver gelatin leaves (6 g)
1/4 cup (1 3/4 oz./50 g) superfine (caster) sugar (1)
2 tbsp. water
1 tbsp. (15 ml) lemon juice
1 3/4 tsp. (5 g) vegetable carbon
Pinch of unrefined sea salt
Scant 1/4 cup (50 ml) whipping cream
5/8 cup (150 ml) sharp olive oil
3 1/4 oz. (90 g) egg whites
1/4 cup (1 3/4 oz./50 g) superfine (caster) sugar (2)
1/4 cup (2 3/4 oz./80 g) syrup from the olive confit

FOR THE OLIVE CRUMBLE

Scant 1/3 cup (1 3/4 oz./50 g) rice flour
1/3 cup + 2 tbsp. (1 3/4 oz./50 g) almond flour
1/4 cup (1 3/4 oz./50 g) superfine (caster) sugar
1/4 cup (50 ml) olive oil
1/2 oz. (15 g) caramelized black olives, reduced to a powder
1 3/4 tsp. (5 g) vegetable carbon

TO SERVE

1/3 cup + 1 1/2 tbsp. (100 ml) lemon leaf kombucha

FOR THE TAPENADE ICE CREAM

Soak the gelatin in a little water. Prepare a syrup with the sugar (1), water, lemon juice, vegetable carbon, and salt. Pour into a bowl sitting inside a mixing bowl filled with ice. Add the cream and drained gelatin and whisk with an electric whisk. As you are whisking and the mixture is cooling, gradually drizzle in the olive oil. In another bowl, whisk the egg whites with the sugar (2) to make a meringue, then gently stir it into the first mixture. Transfer the mixture to the bowl of a Pacojet®. Just before pacotizing, add the olive confit syrup.

FOR THE OLIVE CRUMBLE

Preheat the oven to 340°F (170°C/gas 4). Place all the ingredients in the bowl of a stand mixer fitted with the paddle attachment and knead. Crumble the mixture onto a silicone baking mat, then bake in the oven for 10–12 minutes.

TO SERVE

Arrange the lemon cream, lemon brunoise, and a few confit olives and caramelized olives in a dish. Add the olive crumble and a piece of the nori and olive cristalline. Cover everything with the black olive veil. Just before serving, add some tapenade ice cream and pour a little kombucha into the dish.

CITRUS BOUILLON, **SNOW PEA**, AND SHRIMP

SERVES 4

FOR THE HERB OIL
3 1/2 oz. (100 g) parsley
1 3/4 oz. (50 g) chives
1 oz. (30 g) cilantro (fresh coriander)
1/3 oz. (10 g) dill
1/3 oz. (10 g) tarragon
2 1/2 cups (600 ml) sunflower oil

FOR THE SNOW PEA (MANGETOUT) VEIL
1 silver gelatin leaf (3 g)
3/4 cup + 1 tbsp. (190 ml) cucumber juice
1 1/2 tsp. (3 g) agar-agar powder
7 oz. (200 g) snow peas (mangetout)
3 1/2 oz. (100 g) Lardo di Colonnata

FOR THE SHRIMP (PRAWN) TARTARE
4 1/4 oz. (120 g) San Remo shrimp (prawns)
3/4 oz. (20 g) cucumber (about 2 tsp. diced)
1 3/4 oz. (50 g) avocado (1/3 cup diced)
Olive oil
A few drops of lime juice
Unrefined sea salt

FOR THE CITRUS BOUILLON
1 Granny Smith apple
6 green tomatillos
1/2 cucumber
1/2 white onion
1 serrano chile pepper
1/2 garlic clove
1 oz. (30 g) cilantro (fresh coriander)
Juice of 6 limes
A few drops of yuzu juice
Unrefined sea salt

TO SERVE
20 cilantro (coriander) flowers
Lime gel (see page 207)
Chile oil
Olive oil

FOR THE HERB OIL

Blanch the herbs in boiling water for 1 minute. Cool in iced water. Squeeze the herbs to remove as much water as possible. In a Thermomix®, blend the blanched herbs and the sunflower oil for 10 minutes at 158°F (70°C). Pour the oil into a container and let infuse overnight in the refrigerator. The following day, strain it through a Superbag®, without pressing it. Pour the strained oil into a pipette and set aside in the refrigerator.

FOR THE SNOW PEA (MANGETOUT) VEIL

Soak the gelatin in a little water. In a saucepan, boil the cucumber juice with the agar-agar for 2 minutes, whisking continuously. Remove from the heat and add the drained gelatin. Mix well to dissolve the gelatin, then, using a piston funnel, spread the mixture onto cold marble. Once cold, cut into 2 1/2 x 1 1/2 in. (7 x 4 cm) rectangles. Set aside in the refrigerator.

Wash and trim the snow peas (mangetout) and cut lengthwise into 1/8 in. (3 mm) slices. Using a meat slicer, cut the lard into 1/8 in. (3 mm) slices, then cut each slice into 1/6 in. (4 mm) thick sticks.

Lay the pieces of snow pea and lard next to each other, alternating them, on the cucumber veil. Trim the edges.

FOR THE SHRIMP (PRAWN) TARTARE

Remove the heads from the shrimp (prawns), reserving the juice from the heads and setting it aside in the refrigerator. Peel the shrimp, then finely dice them. Mix with the finely diced cucumber and crushed avocado. Season with olive oil, lime juice, and salt.

FOR THE CITRUS BOUILLON

Peel, seed, and chop the ingredients as necessary, then blend with the lime juice in a Vitamix®. Strain through a chinois, pressing down using a ladle. Season with the yuzu juice and salt, then strain through a Superbag®.

TO SERVE

Place a tablespoon of the shrimp tartare in the center of a dish. Cover with the snow pea veil.

Garnish with the cilantro (coriander) flowers and some dots of lime gel. Pour the citrus bouillon around the edge and add a few drops of the herb, chile, and olive oils.

FRUITS —— SUMMER P. 172

BELL PEPPER
TORTELLINI AND OCTOPUS

SERVES 4

FOR THE OCTOPUS
1 octopus, weighing 6 1/2–9 lb. (3–4 kg)
1 carrot
1 onion
2 bay leaves
Peppercorns

FOR THE RED BELL PEPPER GLAZE
5 oz. (150 g) red bell pepper
4 1/4 cups (1 L) water
2 tsp. soy sauce
1 tsp. colatura di alici
(Italian fermented anchovy sauce)
3/4 tsp. honey

FOR THE HAM CONSOMMÉ
2 1/4 lb. (1 kg) chicken carcasses
1 lb. 2 oz. (500 g) ham bones
10 1/2 oz. (300 g) raw, cured ham

FOR CLARIFYING THE BOUILLON
1/3 cup + 1 1/2 tbsp. (100 ml) lean pork
2 1/4 oz. (60 g) egg white
4 1/4 cups (1 L) ham consommé (see above)

FOR THE PASTA DOUGH
1 red bell pepper
4 tsp. (1/3 oz./10 g) confectioners' (icing) sugar
1 1/4 tsp. (4 g) cornstarch (cornflour)
1 tsp. (3 g) xanthan gum

FOR THE OCTOPUS

Clean the octopus, removing any dirt from the tentacles, entrails, and mouth. Freeze the octopus for 1 week to break down the fibers.
Remove the octopus from the freezer and let thaw. Meanwhile, peel the carrot and onion and dice finely. Place the carrot, onion, bay leaves, and a few peppercorns in a large saucepan and cover with water. Bring to a boil, then add the octopus and let cook for 45 minutes–1 hour. Meanwhile, make the red bell pepper glaze (see below). Once the octopus is cooked, drain and let cool.
Remove the head. Cover the tentacles with the red bell pepper glaze and finish cooking on the grill (barbecue) for about 5 minutes on each side. Once cooked, remove from the grill and cut the tentacles into 1 in. (2.5 cm) pieces. Set aside.

FOR THE RED BELL PEPPER GLAZE

Remove the seeds and core from the pepper and roughly dice the flesh. In a saucepan, boil the pepper for 5 minutes. Drain, then blend in a Vitamix® with the remaining ingredients until smooth. Strain through a chinois.

FOR THE HAM CONSOMMÉ

Roast the chicken carcasses and ham bones in the oven at 350°F (175°C/gas 4) for 30 minutes. Once browned, transfer them to a large saucepan and fill with water. Bring to a boil, then reduce the heat and cook over low heat for 30 minutes. Strain, then return the stock to the pan and add the ham, cut into large cubes. Let macerate for 2 hours at 185°F (85°C). Strain, then set aside in the refrigerator.

FOR CLARIFYING THE BOUILLON

Chop the pork and mix in a food processor with the egg white until combined and smooth. In a saucepan, mix with the cold ham consommé, then gradually increase the heat to clarify. Strain through a chinois lined with paper towels. Set aside 7/8 cup (200 ml) of the bouillon for serving.

FOR THE PASTA DOUGH

Char the bell pepper all over on the grill. Let cool in a covered container. Once cold, peel it and remove the core and seeds.
Preheat the oven to 340°F (170°C/gas 4). In a Thermomix®, blend 6 1/2 oz. (175 g) of the bell pepper flesh with all the remaining ingredients at high speed until smooth. Transfer the mixture to a saucepan and heat to 175°F (80°C), whisking continuously. On a silicone baking mat, roll out the pasta dough onto a template of 20 circles of 2 in. (5 cm) in diameter and bake in the oven for 5 minutes. The disks should be dry but remain supple.

FOR THE FILLING
1 lb. 2 oz. (500 g) pork shoulder
8 cups (2 L) pork stock
1 red bell pepper
1/2 onion
2 tsp. (1/3 oz./10 g) smoked paprika
Scant 1/4 cup (50 ml) meat cooking juices
Olive oil
Modena balsamic vinegar
Unrefined sea salt

FOR THE RED BELL PEPPER SQUARES
1 red bell pepper

FOR THE VEAL BRISKET
3/4 oz. (20 g) veal brisket
2 cups + 1 tbsp. (500 ml) water

FOR THE CHILE OIL
1 1/4 cups (300 ml) grapeseed oil
1 3/4 oz. (50 g) red chile pepper

FOR THE FILLING

Place the pork shoulder in a roasting pan, cover with the pork stock, and cook in the oven at 340°F (170°C/gas 4) for 1 hour. Once the meat is cooked, let it cool, then shred it.
Remove the seeds and core from the bell pepper, peel the onion, and dice both finely. Sweat in a saucepan with some olive oil and a little salt. Once the vegetables are well cooked, mix them in a food processor. Let cool.
In a mixing bowl, stir together the shredded pork, the puréed vegetables, smoked paprika, meat cooking juices, a drizzle of balsamic vinegar, and some salt. Set aside.

TO MAKE THE TORTELLINI

Place half a teaspoon of filling in the center of each pasta disk. Fold in half and press the edges with your fingers to seal. If the dough is too dry, brush a little water around the edges. Hold the half-moon with the thumb and index finger of each hand, push the filling back slightly with your thumbs, then bring the two points together. Press and seal to make tortellini.

FOR THE RED BELL PEPPER SQUARES

Char the bell pepper all over on the grill. Let cool in a covered container. Once cold, peel it and remove the core and seeds. Cut into 1 in. (2.5 cm) squares.

FOR THE VEAL BRISKET

Place the brisket in a saucepan, cover with the water, and bring to a boil. Reduce the heat and simmer over low heat until cooked, about 1 hour 30 minutes. Remove from the saucepan and let cool. Then cut into 1 in. (2.5 cm) cubes.

FOR THE CHILE OIL

In a small saucepan, heat the oil to 185°F (85°C), then remove from the heat and add the whole chile pepper. Let infuse for at least 1 hour. Strain the oil and set aside in a pipette.

TO SERVE

Place three red bell pepper squares and three veal cubes in a dish. Add three pieces of the glazed octopus and five red pepper tortellini. Top with a few drops of chile oil, then finish by pouring over the hot consommé.

ZUCCHINI, EGGPLANT, AND TOMATO TART

MAKES ONE 8 IN. (20 CM) DIAMETER TART

FOR THE PUFF PASTRY SHELL (CASE)

8 1/3 cups (2 1/4 lb./1 kg) pastry (soft) flour
2 cups + 1 tbsp. (500 ml) water
3/4 cup + 2 tbsp. (7 oz./200 g) softened butter
4 tsp. (3/4 oz./20 g) salt
1 lb. 10 oz. (750 g) sheet butter (12 x 15 in./30 x 40 cm)

FOR THE EGGPLANT (AUBERGINE) PURÉE

2 eggplants (aubergines)
Salt

FOR THE VEGETABLE ROSE

1 eggplant (aubergine)
1 green zucchini (courgette)
1 yellow zucchini (courgette)
1 trumpet zucchini (courgette)
20 tomato confit petals
Parmesan shavings
Olive oil

FOR THE PROVENÇAL SAUCE

1 3/4 oz. (50 g) tomato confit
7 oz. (200 g) preserved lemon
3 1/2 oz. (100 g) Taggiasca olives, pitted
1 3/4 oz. (50 g) small capers in vinegar
1/3 cup + 1 1/2 tbsp. (100 ml) veal stock

FOR THE PUFF PASTRY SHELL (CASE)

Knead the flour with the water, softened butter, and salt to obtain a smooth dough. Let rest for 20–30 minutes in the refrigerator.
Preheat the oven to 340°F (170°C/gas 4). Roll out the dough into a 20 x 24 in. (50 x 60 cm) rectangle and place the very cold sheet of butter in the center. Next, fold into three, then roll out again, turn and repeat six times.
Roll out to a thickness of 1/8 in. (3 mm), cut out a 9 1/2 in. (24 cm) diameter circle and line an 8 in. (20 cm) diameter pie plate (tart tin). Cover with foil and add weights (rice or lentils). Chill before blind baking in the oven for 15 minutes. Trim the edge using scissors.

FOR THE EGGPLANT (AUBERGINE) PURÉE

Wash and prick the eggplants (aubergines). Cook them in a dry oven at 500°F (260°C/gas 9) for about 15 minutes. Remove the flesh, discarding the skins, and mix it in a Vitamix® with a little salt. The purée should be very smooth. Let cool, then transfer the purée to a pastry (piping) bag.

FOR THE VEGETABLE ROSE

Wash the vegetables and, using a mandoline, cut them into 1/8 in. (3 mm) slices. In a griddle pan, with a drizzle of olive oil, grill the eggplant strips on both sides so that the grill marks are visible. Leave the zucchini (courgette) raw.
In an 8 in. (20 cm) diameter presentation ring, create a rose with the vegetable slices, alternating the different colors. Finally, insert the tomato confit petals.

FOR THE PROVENÇAL SAUCE

Chop the tomatoes, lemons, and olives into 1/4 in. (5 mm) cubes. Drain the capers. Heat the veal stock and stir in the other ingredients. Set aside.

TO ASSEMBLE AND SERVE

Arrange the Parmesan shavings over the bottom of the tart shell. Cover with the eggplant purée. Slide the vegetable rose on to a spatula and lay it carefully on the eggplant purée.
Bake in the oven at 355°F (180°C/gas 4) for 15 minutes to finish cooking.
Cut the hot tart into slices and serve with a little of the Provençal sauce.

RASPBERRIES AND VERBENA

SERVES 4

FOR THE PEACH COMPOTE
10 1/2 oz. (300 g) flat peaches
2 1/2 tbsp. (1 oz./30 g) superfine (caster) sugar
2 tsp. lemon juice
2 3/4 oz. (75 g) raspberries

FOR THE RASPBERRY CRISTALLINE
1 lb. 2 oz. (500 g) raspberries
2 cups + 1 tbsp. (500 ml) water

FOR THE PEACH AND VERBENA INFUSION
1/4 cup (1 3/4 oz./50 g) superfine (caster) sugar
Scant 1/4 cup (50 ml) water
7 oz. (200 g) peach skins
1 1/2 cups (350 ml) water
1/3 oz. (10 g) verbena leaves

FOR THE GOAT MILK ICE CREAM
1 cup + 2 1/2 tbsp. (275 ml) goat milk
1/3 cup (86 ml) whipping cream
1/3 cup + 2 tbsp. (2 1/2 oz./70 g) dextrose
2 3/4 tbsp. (3/4 oz./21 g) powdered milk
2 tsp. inverted sugar syrup
2 tbsp. (1 oz./25 g) superfine (caster) sugar
3/4 tsp. (2 g) carob flour

TO SERVE
48 fresh raspberries
12 small sprigs of verbena flowers

FOR THE PEACH COMPOTE

Peel and stone the peaches and cut the flesh into 1/4 in. (5 mm) strips. Reserve the skins for making the infusion. In a saucepan, cook the peaches with the sugar and lemon juice over low heat for 25 minutes. Let cool, then add the raspberries, mixing to break them up a bit. Set aside in the refrigerator.

FOR THE RASPBERRY CRISTALLINE

In a saucepan, boil the raspberries with the water. Strain through a Superbag® to obtain clear, impurity-free raspberry water. Pour into 2 in. (5 cm) diameter circular silicone molds and freeze to obtain four 1/6 in. (4 mm) thick disks. Store in the freezer until the last minute.

FOR THE PEACH AND VERBENA INFUSION

In a saucepan, make a syrup with the sugar and the scant 1/4 cup (50 ml) water. Stir in the remaining ingredients and bring to a boil. Let infuse for 30 minutes. Strain through a chinois. Set aside in the refrigerator to serve very cold.

FOR THE GOAT MILK ICE CREAM

In a saucepan, stir the milk with the cream, dextrose, powdered milk, and inverted sugar syrup. Heat to 104°F (40°C), then stir in the sugar mixed with the carob flour. Heat to 185°F (85°C), then cool to 39°F (4°C) and let mature overnight in the refrigerator. Churn in an ice cream maker.

TO SERVE

In a dish, arrange 12 fresh raspberries in a circle the same size as the raspberry cristalline. Place the peach compote in the middle of this circle and add a scoop of goat milk ice cream in the center. Cover everything with the raspberry cristalline. Decorate with the verbena flowers. Pour in the peach and verbena infusion just before serving.

BUTTERNUT **SQUASH** AND FISH TARTARE

SERVES 4

FOR THE FISH TARTARE
1 white fish fillet (dentex, sea bream, bass, or other sustainable fish from your region), weighing 10 1/2 oz. (300 g)
2 tbsp. (3/4 oz./20 g) finely diced shallot
1/3 cup + 2 tbsp. (3/4 oz./20 g) snipped chives
Lemon juice
Lemon zest
Olive oil
Salt and pepper

FOR THE PUMPKIN SEED PRALINE
1 1/2 cups (3 1/2 oz./100 g) pumpkin seeds
Pumpkinseed oil

FOR THE MUSTARD ICE CREAM
1 cup + 1 tbsp. (250 ml) whole milk
3/8 cup (3 1/4 oz./90 g) yellow mustard
2 tbsp. (1 oz./30 g) seed-style mustard
2/3 tsp. (5 g) glucose syrup
1/2 tsp. (2.5 g) fleur de sel
2 1/4 oz. (60 g) egg yolk

FOR THE SQUASH VINAIGRETTE
1 lb. 2 oz. (500 g) butternut squash
1 small turmeric root
Juice of 1 lemon
Pumpkinseed oil
Salt

FOR THE BUTTERNUT VEIL
1 butternut squash
4 1/4 cups (1 L) water
5/8 cup (150 ml) cider vinegar
1 tsp. superfine (caster) sugar
Unrefined sea salt
Peppercorns

FOR THE BUTTERNUT PURÉE
The flesh from 1 butternut squash
1/3 cup + 1 1/2 tbsp. (100 g) butter
1/2 onion, chopped
Unrefined sea salt

FOR THE FISH TARTARE

Finely dice the fish and mix with the chopped shallot and chives and season to taste with lemon juice and zest, olive oil, salt, and pepper. Set aside in the refrigerator.

FOR THE PUMPKIN SEED PRALINE

Preheat the oven to 340°F (170°C/gas 4), then toast the pumpkin seeds for 10 minutes. In a Thermomix®, mix the toasted pumpkin seeds with a little pumpkinseed oil until smooth. Transfer to a pastry (piping) bag.

FOR THE MUSTARD ICE CREAM

In a Thermomix®, heat the milk with the yellow and seed-style mustards, glucose syrup, and fleur de sel to 104°F (40°C). Gradually add the egg yolk and raise the temperature to 180°F (82°C). Strain through a sieve, then freeze in a Pacojet® tray. Once the mixture is frozen, pacotize. Spread the ice cream out on a baking sheet lined with a silicone baking mat to 1/8 in. (3 mm) thick. Freeze again, then, using a 1 1/2 in. (4 cm) diameter cookie (pastry) cutter, cut out disks. Store in a sealed container in the freezer.

FOR THE SQUASH VINAIGRETTE

Peel the squash and cut the flesh into small pieces. Peel the turmeric root. Place both in a juicer and recover the juices. Strain through a chinois.
Make a vinaigrette with the squash and turmeric juice, the lemon juice, pumpkinseed oil, and salt.

FOR THE BUTTERNUT VEIL

Peel the butternut squash and, using a Japanese turning slicer, thinly slice the top (seedless) part. Use a tear-shaped cookie cutter to cut out "petals" from the strips. In a saucepan, boil the water with the vinegar, sugar, a little salt, and a few peppercorns. Soak the butternut petals in the mixture for about 5–7 minutes. They should be slightly crunchy. Drain the petals and stick them together to form a rosette. Set aside in the refrigerator between two sheets of parchment (baking) paper.

FOR THE BUTTERNUT PURÉE

Cut the butternut flesh into thin slices using a mandoline. In a saucepan, melt the butter, then add the butternut slices and chopped onion and cook for 10 minutes. When the butternut begins to sweat, cover with parchment paper and cook over low heat for a further 30 minutes. Season with salt. Remove the paper and stir to dry the purée. Remove from the heat and blend in a Vitamix®. Let cool then transfer to a pipette.

TO SERVE

Place a dot of pumpkinseed praline in the center of a high-sided dinner plate. Using a 1 1/4 in. (3 cm) diameter presentation ring, place the fish tartare in the center. Add a few dots of the butternut purée, then top with the mustard ice cream and cover with the butternut veil. Finish by pouring the squash vinaigrette around the edge.

FRUITS —— FALL P. 182

FOIE GRAS AND **PORCINI MUSHROOMS** FROM THE COL DE TENDE

SERVES 4

FOR THE FOIE GRAS
2 foie gras escalopes

FOR THE FOIE GRAS FAT
The trimmings from the foie gras

FOR THE PORCINI MUSHROOMS
2 porcini mushrooms
1 garlic clove
1 thyme sprig
Scant 1/4 cup (1 3/4 oz./50 g) butter
Olive oil
Fleur de sel

FOR THE MUSHROOM CONSOMMÉ
3 cups + 2 tbsp. (750 ml) water
1/2 oz. (15 g) kombu (dried kelp)
1 1/2 oz. (45 g) dried porcini mushrooms
2 tsp. soy sauce
1/8 oz. (3 g) kuzu
Salt

TO SERVE
1 fresh porcini mushroom
20 chickweed sprouts

FOR THE FOIE GRAS

Cook the foie gras escalopes in a griddle pan over low heat for 3 minutes on each side so that the grill marks are visible. Let rest for 5 minutes before slicing diagonally into slices about 1/2 in. (1 cm) thick.

FOR THE FOIE GRAS FAT

Place all the foie gras trimmings in a saucepan and melt over low heat. Strain, and collect the fat. Set aside.

FOR THE PORCINI MUSHROOMS

Clean the mushrooms and turn them using a small knife. Cut them in half. Finely chop the garlic and strip the leaves from the thyme sprig. Heat them in a skillet (frying pan) with a drizzle of olive oil. Cook the porcini mushrooms, cut size down, without browning them too much. Finish cooking by basting them with the hot melted butter. Season with a little fleur de sel.

FOR THE MUSHROOM CONSOMMÉ

In a saucepan, mix the water, kombu, and dried porcini mushrooms and let infuse for 2 hours at 140°F (60°C). Strain through a Superbag®. Season with salt and a little soy sauce, then add texture with a little kuzu.

TO SERVE

Clean the mushroom and turn it using a small knife. Slice thinly using a mandoline. In a dish, place a slice of foie gras on the left and a porcini mushroom half on the right. Pour 2 tablespoons of mushroom consommé around the edge. Finish with a few drops of foie gras fat and the thin slices of fresh porcini mushroom. Garnish with five chickweed sprouts to finish.

FRUITS —— FALL P. 184

MALLARD AND **QUINCE** TERRINE

SERVES 6

FOR THE MALLARD
1 mallard crown
1 tbsp. clarified butter
Olive oil
Fleur de sel

FOR THE QUINCE TERRINE
2 1/4 lb. (1 kg) quinces
1/3 cup + 2 tbsp. (3 1/2 oz./100 g) clarified butter
Unrefined sea salt

FOR THE STUFFED OLIVES
1/3 cup (1 3/4 oz./50 g) pistachios
3/4 cup (2 3/4 oz./75 g) grated Parmesan
1/3 cup (80 ml) olive oil
1 oz. (30 g) green olives, pitted
3 1/2 oz. (100 g) basil
6 large green olives
Unrefined sea salt

FOR THE QUINCE GASTRIQUE
The peel from the quinces used for the terrine
4 1/4 cups (1 L) water
1/4 oz. (5 g) dried hibiscus flowers

FOR THE MALLARD

In a skillet (frying pan) brown the mallard crown, bone side down, with a drizzle of olive oil over low heat for 15 minutes. Turn the mallard onto one side and cook for 15 minutes, then turn onto the other side and cook for a further 15 minutes. Finish by browning the skin by pressing it against the pan. Let rest before carving.
Remove the mallard breast fillets and cut each into three pieces lengthwise. Brush with the clarified butter and sprinkle with a few grains of fleur de sel.

FOR THE QUINCE TERRINE

Preheat the oven to 355°F (180°C/gas 4). Wash and peel the quinces, discarding the seeds but reserving the peel for the gastrique. Allow to oxidize to obtain a deep red color.
Using a mandoline, cut into very thin (2 mm) slices. Line a lidded terrine dish in both directions with parchment (baking) paper, allowing enough overhang on each side to fold over the top. Layer slices of quince on top of each other to fill the mold. Brush each layer with a little clarified butter to stick them together, and season every other layer with a little salt. Fold the edges of the parchment paper over the top of the terrine, then cover with the lid. Bake in the oven for 45 minutes. Remove from the oven, press down on the top, then let cool in the mold.
Once the terrine is cold, remove it from the mold and cut into slices the same thickness and size as the slices of duck breast.

FOR THE STUFFED OLIVES

In a blender, mix the pistachios with the Parmesan and olive oil. Add the pitted green olives and the basil leaves and season with unrefined sea salt. Transfer this pesto to a pastry (piping) bag.
Pit the large olives and fill them with this pesto. Store at room temperature.

FOR THE QUINCE GASTRIQUE

In a blender, blend the quince peel with the water. Pour into a saucepan and add the dried hibiscus flowers. Bring to a boil over low heat to clarify the sauce, then strain to remove any impurities. Reduce the sauce until it has the consistency of caramel.

FRUITS —— FALL P. 186

FOR THE MALLARD GRAVY

MALLARD STOCK
6 1/2 lb. (3 kg) mallard carcasses

GRAVY
3 1/4 lb. (1.5 kg) mallard legs
1 carrot
1 celery stalk
1/2 onion
Olive oil

TO SERVE
6 red shiso sprouts

FOR THE MALLARD STOCK

Place the mallard carcasses in a baking pan and roast them in the oven at 355°F (180°C/gas 4) for 40 minutes. Once they are browned, remove the fat and transfer the carcasses to a large saucepan. Cover with cold water and cook over low heat for 8 hours. Strain. Set aside in the refrigerator and when cold, skim off the fat.

FOR THE MALLARD GRAVY

Cut the mallard legs into small pieces. In a sauté pan, brown the mallard in a little olive oil. Once browned, remove from the pan and remove the fat. Finely chop the carrot, celery, and half onion, then sweat the diced vegetables in a skillet.
Place the browned mallard meat and vegetables in a large saucepan and pour over the duck stock. Let reduce for 3 hours, then strain and let reduce for a further 30 minutes until the gravy has a velvety texture. Skim off the fat regularly using a skimming spoon.
Strain through a chinois, then through a Superbag®. Set aside in the refrigerator and, when cold, skim off the fat.

TO SERVE

Place a slice of mallard in a dish and lay a slice of terrine to the left of it, touching each other. On the side, add a little of each sauce. Finish with a stuffed olive and garnish with a shiso sprout.

PRICKLY PEAR AND YUZU

SERVES 4

FOR THE YUZU GANACHE
3 tbsp. (45 ml) whipping cream (1)
3/4 tsp. (5 g) glucose syrup
3/4 tsp. (5 g) inverted sugar syrup
2 1/4 oz. (60 g) white chocolate
3/8 cup (90 ml) whipping cream (2)
4 tsp. (20 ml) yuzu juice

FOR THE DRIED PRICKLY PEAR
1 prickly pear

FOR THE YELLOW PRICKLY PEAR SORBET
14 oz. (400 g) yellow prickly pears (for 1 2/3 cups/400 ml juice)
2 tbsp. water
2/3 cup (3 1/2 oz./100 g) dextrose
3 tbsp. (1 1/4 oz./35 g) superfine (caster) sugar
1 tsp. (2.5 g) carob flour

FOR THE RED PRICKLY PEAR SORBET
14 oz. (400 g) red prickly pears (for 1 2/3 cups/400 ml juice)
2 tbsp. water
2/3 cup (3 1/2 oz./100 g) dextrose
3 tbsp. (1 1/4 oz./35 g) superfine (caster) sugar
1 tsp. (2.5 g) carob flour

TO SERVE
1 caviar lime

FOR THE YUZU GANACHE

In a saucepan, heat the cream (1), glucose syrup, and inverted sugar syrup to 140°F (60°C). Break the white chocolate into pieces and place in a bowl. Pour the hot mixture over the chocolate, stir, then let cool to 95°F (35°C). Once at this temperature, add the cold cream (2) and stir, but do not whisk.
Let rest in the refrigerator for 4–6 hours. Add the yuzu juice and whisk vigorously to obtain a ganache. Set aside in the refrigerator.

FOR THE DRIED PRICKLY PEAR

Wearing gloves, carefully peel the prickly pear. Remove the flesh, discarding the seeds, and reserve the outer peel. Dry the flesh in a desiccator at 122°F (50°C) for 24 hours.
Cut the dried flesh into 1/2 in. (1 cm) squares.

FOR THE YELLOW PRICKLY PEAR SORBET

Wearing gloves, carefully peel the prickly pears. Use a juicer to obtain 1 cup + 1 tbsp. (250 ml) of juice.
In a saucepan, heat the water with a scant 1/4 cup (50 ml) of the juice, then stir in the dextrose, sugar, and carob flour. Cook until the mixture reaches 185°F (85°C), then cool to 39°F (4°C) and let mature overnight in the refrigerator. Churn in an ice cream maker.

FOR THE RED PRICKLY PEAR SORBET

Wearing gloves, carefully peel the prickly pears. Use a juicer to obtain 1 cup + 1 tbsp. (250 ml) of juice.
In a saucepan, heat the water with a scant 1/4 cup (50 ml) of the juice, then stir in the dextrose, sugar, and carob flour. Cook until the mixture reaches 185°F (85°C), then cool to 39°F (4°C) and let mature overnight in the refrigerator. Churn in an ice cream maker.

TO SERVE

Cut open the caviar lime. Remove the seeds and set them aside in the refrigerator.
In a stainless-steel container, mix a few tablespoons each of the red and yellow sorbets to create a marble effect. Set aside in the freezer at 9°F (-13°C).
Place three pieces of dried prickly pear in a dish and cover them with a quenelle of the yuzu ganache. Add a teaspoon of the caviar lime seeds, then top everything with a quenelle of the marbled prickly pear sorbet.

FRUITS —— FALL P. 190

CHIA **CITRON**, AND VENISON TARTARE

SERVES 10

FOR THE CHIA TACOS
2 1/2 tbsp. (oz./25 g) chia seeds
1/3 cup + 1 1/2 tbsp. (100 ml) water
1/4 tsp. (4 g) salt
1 1/2 tbsp. (1/3 oz./10 g) glucose powder
4 1/4 cups (1 L) sunflower oil

FOR THE VENISON TARTARE
7 oz. (200 g) lean venison
2 tbsp. (3/4 oz./20 g) finely diced shallot
2 anchovy fillets, chopped
1 oz. (30 g) tomato confit, chopped
1/3 cup (1/2 oz./15 g) snipped chives
1 tbsp. soy sauce
Voatsiperifery (Madagascar wild) pepper
Olive oil
Lemon zest
Unrefined sea salt

FOR THE PRESERVED CITRON
7 oz. (200 g) preserved citron

FOR THE CHIA TACOS

In a saucepan, boil all the ingredients except the sunflower oil, then let rest for a few minutes to hydrate the chia seeds. Spread the dough in a thin layer in ten 3/4 in. (2 cm) diameter round molds on a silicone baking mat.
Cover with another silicone baking mat and place in a desiccator at 122°F (50°C) for 4 hours. Then fry at 355°F (180°C) for a few seconds and shape into tacos using a metal tube. Drain on paper towels then return the tacos to the desiccator until ready to serve.

FOR THE VENISON TARTARE

Finely chop the meat and mix with the shallot, anchovy, tomato confit, chives, and soy sauce. Season to taste with Voatsiperifery (Madagascar wild) pepper, olive oil, lemon zest, and unrefined sea salt. Set aside in the refrigerator.

FOR THE PRESERVED CITRON

Supreme the citron and cut flesh into 1/2 in. (1 cm) cubes, then into thin strips. Set aside.

TO SERVE

Fill the tacos with the venison tartare and garnish with the strips of preserved citron.

FISH OF THE DAY AND **SUDACHI** SAUCE

SERVES 4

FOR THE FISH
1 bream or mahi-mahi fillet
(or other sustainable fish
from your region) 13–14 oz. (370–400 g)
4 tsp. (3/4 oz./20 g) clarified butter

FOR THE SUDACHI SAUCE
1 oz. (25 g) celery root (celeriac)
2 1/2 tbsp. (1 1/4 oz./35 g) trout roe
3 tbsp. (1 3/4 oz./50 g) tapioca
2 cups + 1 tbsp. (500 ml) water
2 tbsp. (30 ml) wild sudachi juice
2 sticks + 2 tbsp. (8 3/4 oz./250 g) cold butter
1 tbsp. (1/4 oz./5 g) finely sliced scallion
(green onion)
2 tbsp. (5 g) snipped chives
Unrefined sea salt

TO SERVE
12 cilantro (coriander) flowers

FOR THE FISH

Cook the fish in a combi oven at 165°F (75°C) with 10% humidity for 8 minutes. Remove the skin and cut the fish into 3 1/4 oz. (90 g) portions. Brush with the clarified butter.

FOR THE SUDACHI SAUCE

Peel, then finely dice the celery root (celeriac). Set aside in a container of cold water. Wash the trout roe in cold water, then drain.
Cook the tapioca in the salted boiling water for 3 minutes. Strain through a chinois, then set aside in a container of cold water. Leave in the refrigerator until the tapioca has puffed up.
In a skillet (frying pan), heat the sudachi juice with a pinch of salt. Dice the butter and add it to the pan a little at the time, whisking it in. Continue to whisk to obtain a *beurre monté*. The sauce should have a creamy consistency.
Stir in the trout roe, tapioca, celery root (celeriac), scallion, and chives. Season with a little sudachi juice and salt, if needed.

TO SERVE

Place the fish on a plate and cover with the sudachi sauce. Garnish with the cilantro (coriander) flowers.

FRUITS —— WINTER P. 192, P. 194

SQUAB AND **BANANA FROM THE GARDEN**

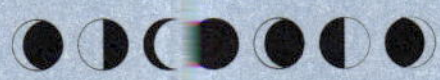

SERVES 4

— FIRST DISH

FOR THE SQUAB
2 squabs
1/3 cup + 2 tbsp. (3 1/2 oz./100 g) butter, for basting
4 tsp. (20 ml) clarified butter, for brushing
Fleur de sel

FOR THE CARAMELIZED BANANA
1 underripe banana
1/3 cup + 1 tsp. (2 3/4 oz./80 g) butter
2 1/2 tbsp. (1 oz./30 g) muscovado sugar
1 star anise
1 cinnamon stick
3 green cardamom pods

FOR THE SHALLOT AND BLACK GARLIC CONDIMENT
2 heads (3 1/2 oz./100 g) black garlic
1 head (1 3/4 oz./50 g) white garlic
4 1/4 cups (1 L) cold water
1/3 cup (80 ml) whole milk
2 tbsp. (1 oz./30 g) squid ink
2 3/4 oz. (80 g) shallot
Knob of butter
Unrefined sea salt

—— FIRST DISH

FOR THE SQUAB

Clean the squabs by removing the head, first part of the wings, and entrails. Remove the wishbone, which, with the neck, will serve to make the pigeon gravy. Reserve the hearts and livers. Truss the squabs without using a needle. Ideally, let mature for a few days in the refrigerator.
Place the squabs on their backs in a skillet (frying pan) and brown over low heat. Once the backs are brown, turn and cook the legs on each side, using a small skewer to keep them in place. The breasts should not come into contact with the pan. Finish cooking the squabs by basting them with the hot butter.
Let rest, then remove the breasts, cut them in half lengthwise, brush them with the clarified butter, and season with a few grains of fleur de sel.

FOR THE CARAMELIZED BANANA

Peel the banana and cut in half, then cut each half in two lengthwise.
In a skillet, heat the butter with the sugar and spices until the sugar has dissolved. Add the pieces of banana and caramelize them over low heat. Once they are colored, remove from the heat and trim the ends to give them the same shape as the squab breasts. Set aside.

FOR THE SHALLOT AND BLACK GARLIC CONDIMENT

Peel the black and white garlic cloves and remove the germ from the white garlic cloves. Blanch the white garlic in water five times, using fresh water each time. Drain.
In a small saucepan, stir together the black garlic, blanched white garlic, and the milk, cook over low heat until creamy, about 15 minutes. Mix to a smooth purée in a blender. Add the squid ink and blend again.
In a skillet, sweat the chopped shallot in the butter. Once it is transparent, stir in the garlic purée. Add a little salt if needed. Keep warm.

FRUITS —— WINTER P. 196

FOR THE PIGEON GRAVY
10 pigeon carcasses
3 1/4 qt. (3 L) water
1 tbsp. pigeon blood
Ground cumin
Madras curry powder
Balsamic vinegar
Olive oil

FOR THE PIGEON GRAVY

Prepare in three stages.
First make the stock. Preheat the oven to 355°F (180°C/gas 4). Place five of the pigeon carcasses in a baking pan and roast them in the oven for 20 minutes. Transfer them to a cooking pot and cover with the water. Cook over low heat for 12 hours. Strain. Let cool then skim off the fat.
Prepare the gravy. Chop the remaining pigeon carcasses into small pieces and, in a saucepan, brown them in olive oil. Remove the carcasses from the pan and set aside. Deglaze the pan with a little water.
Place the browned carcasses, cooking juices, and a third of the prepared stock into another large saucepan. Reduce by half. Continue adding and reducing the stock. Season with 1 teaspoon each of ground cumin and Madras curry powder. Continue cooking over low heat for about 3 hours to concentrate the flavors. Filter and reduce again. (Simmer gently and skim off the fat and impurities regularly.) When the gravy has reached the right consistency, strain it through a Superbag®. Let cool to remove the fat.
Prepare the seasoning. Heat the pigeon gravy and season with a little more curry powder and cumin and some balsamic vinegar. Blend using an immersion blender, adding the pigeon blood for texture. Heat again to cook the blood. Strain and reserve.

TO SERVE

Arrange the squab breast and the caramelized banana side by side in an oval dish. Place a quenelle of the shallot and black garlic condiment to one side. Finish with the pigeon gravy. Serve with a foie gras skewer (see below).

— SECOND DISH

FOR THE FOIE GRAS SKEWERS
1 banana leaf
1 foie gras escalope
2 cooked squab legs
4 tsp. (3/4 oz./20 g) clarified butter
Fleur de sel

—— SECOND DISH

FOR THE FOIE GRAS SKEWERS

Using scissors, cut the banana leaf to make four little skewers.
Grill the foie gras escalope for about 5 minutes on each side. Once cooked, cut into four slices, then shape each slice into a rectangle.
Bone the squab legs. Cut each leg in half.
Thread a rectangle of foie gras and a piece of leg onto each banana leaf skewer. Brush with the clarified butter and season with a few grains of fleur de sel. Gently reheat the squab in the salamander and serve on a separate plate.

MENTON LEMON AND STRACCIATELLA

SERVES 4

FOR THE "GARAVAN" WATER
3 1/2 oz. (100 g) Menton lemon
1 3/4 oz. (50 g) lime
2/3 cup (2 3/4 oz./80 g) superfine (caster) sugar (1)
1 1/2 cups (350 ml) water
3 tbsp. (1 1/4 oz./35 g) superfine (caster) sugar (2)
4 tsp. (20 ml) Menton lemon juice
1 tsp. (2 g) blue spirulina powder

FOR THE GREEN PASTE
4 1/4 cups (1 L) water
3 1/2 oz. (100 g) spinach leaves

FOR THE LEMON LEAVES
1 1/2 oz. (45 g) egg white
1/3 cup (2 1/4 oz./65 g) superfine (caster) sugar
1/2 cup (2 1/4 oz./65 g) all-purpose (plain) flour
2 1/2 tbsp. (1 1/4 oz./35 g) butter
3/4 oz. (20 g) green paste (see above)

FOR THE LIME CREAM
1 1/2 silver gelatin leaves (3.5 g)
5 oz. (150 g) whole eggs
1 3/4 oz. (50 g) egg yolk
3/4 cup (5 oz./150 g) superfine (caster) sugar
1 1/4 tsp. (2.5 g) lime zest
5/8 cup (150 ml) lime juice
3/4 cup (6 1/4 oz./175 g) butter, at room temperature

FOR THE STRACCIATELLA AND LIMONCELLO FOAM
1 1/4 silver gelatin leaves (3.2 g)
10 1/2 oz. (300 g) Stracciatella cheese
1/4 cup (60 ml) limoncello
2 1/2 tbsp. (1 oz./30 g) superfine (caster) sugar

FOR THE "GARAVAN" WATER

Wash the Menton lemon and lime, then slice them very thinly and place them in a stainless-steel container. In a saucepan, boil the sugar (1) and water. Pour this syrup over the citrus slices and let infuse in the refrigerator for 24 hours.
Strain through a chinois into a saucepan, add the sugar (2), and simmer over low heat for 1 hour. Remove from the heat and let cool in the refrigerator. When cold, stir in the Menton lemon juice and the spirulina. Strain through a fine-mesh sieve, then set aside in the refrigerator.

FOR THE GREEN PASTE

Bring the water to a boil in a saucepan, blanch the spinach leaves for 4 minutes, then immediately immerse them in crushed ice. Drain, then blend in a Thermomix®.

FOR THE LEMON LEAVES

Preheat the oven to 355°F (180°C/gas 4). Using a mixer, whisk the egg white with 1/3 oz. (10 g) of the sugar. When the mixture forms stiff peaks, add the remaining sugar, sifted flour, and melted butter. Gently mix together using a spatula, then stir in the green paste. Spread in a thin layer onto a silicone baking mat with a lightly greased leaf-shaped template. Make eight leaves then bake in the oven for 5 minutes. Remove from the oven and weight it down using a stainless-steel baking tray. Once the leaves are cold, store them in an airtight container.

FOR THE LIME CREAM

Soak the gelatin leaves in a little cold water. Using a mixer, beat the eggs with the egg yolks, sugar, and lime zest until foamy. In a saucepan, boil the lime juice, add the drained gelatin and stir until dissolved, then pour over the egg mixture. Continue to whisk. Once it reaches 113°C (45°F), gradually add the butter. Set aside in the refrigerator. Whisk again before use.

FOR THE STRACCIATELLA AND LIMONCELLO FOAM

Soak the gelatin leaves in a little cold water. In a Thermomix®, mix the stracciatella with the limoncello then strain through a chinois to obtain a smooth cream. In a saucepan, heat a third of the limoncello stracciatella. Remove from the heat and add the sugar and the drained gelatin. Stir well with the remaining stracciatella mixture, then set aside in the refrigerator. When it has set, mix using an immersion blender, then transfer to a siphon fitted with two gas cartridges.

FRUITS —— WINTER P. 198

FOR THE GOAT CHEESE SORBET
1/2 cup + 1 tbsp. (132 ml) water
1/3 cup + 2 tbsp. (3 1/4 oz./90 g) superfine (caster) sugar
1 1/4 tsp. (2.5 g) Menton lemon zest
3 tbsp. (1/3 oz./20 g) glucose powder
2 tbsp. (1/2 oz./15 g) powdered milk
1 3/4 tsp. (4 g) carob flour
1 1/3 cups (5 oz./150 g) fresh goat cheese
Scant 1/3 cup (2 3/4 oz./75 g) plain (natural) matsoni yogurt

FOR THE MENTON LEMON SORBET
3/4 cup + 2 tbsp. (6 1/2 oz./180 g) superfine (caster) sugar
7/8 cup (200 ml) water
1/4 cup (60 ml) heavy (double) cream
5/8 cup (150 ml) Menton lemon juice
3/4 tsp. (1.5 g) Menton lemon zest

FOR THE PRESERVED MENTON LEMONS
4 Menton lemons
2 1/2 cups (1 lb. 2 oz./500 g) superfine (caster) sugar
2 cups + 2 tbsp. (500 ml) water (for the syrup)

FOR THE GOAT CHEESE SORBET

In a saucepan, boil the water with the sugar, lemon zest, glucose powder, powdered milk, and carob flour. Remove from the heat and let mature in the refrigerator for 24 hours.
Mix this base with the goat cheese and matsoni yogurt, transfer to a Pacojet® bowl and place in the freezer. Pacotize before use.

FOR THE MENTON LEMON SORBET

In a saucepan, make a syrup with the sugar and water. Let cool, then stir in the cream and lemon juice and zest. Transfer to a Pacojet® bowl and place in the freezer. Pacotize twice before use.

FOR THE MENTON LEMON PRESERVE

Blanch the lemons ten times, using fresh water each time. Make an incision on the underside of the lemons, then, using a melon baller, carefully scoop out the juice and pulp without breaking the peel.
Make a syrup with the sugar and water. Add the lemons and heat to 185°F (85°C), then remove from the heat and let cool. Repeat the operation until there is no more flesh or zest in the lemons. Store the whole preserved lemons in the syrup in the refrigerator.

TO SERVE

Fill a preserved lemon with a little of the lime cream, then add a tablespoon of each sorbet and the stracciatella and limoncello foam. Place in a dish. Stick two lemon leaves into the top, then pour the "Garavan" water around the edge.

FRUITS —— WINTER P. 198

ROOTS

SPRING

Turnip and Shellfish Tartlet, page 202
Kohlrabi and Shellfish, page 203
Carrot, Kumquat, and Pork Belly Terrine, page 204
Wasabi and Green Apple, page 206

SUMMER

Menton Onion, Caramote Shrimp, and Red Shiso, page 207
New Potato Ragout, page 209
Fish, Licorice, and Black Garlic, page 210
Turmeric and Apricot, page 211

FALL

Beet and Caviar, page 212
Celery Root and Squid Tagliatelle, page 213
Assorted Potato Gnocchi, page 214
Ginger and Penja White Pepper, page 216

WINTER

Onion and Comté Cube, page 218
Assorted Radish, Fish, and Citrus Fruit Rosette, page 219
Fish of the Day and Leeks, page 220
Sunchoke Churros, page 222

LEAVES

SPRING

Celtuce, Stracciatella, and Caviar, page 223
Garden Salad and Vermouth Sauce, page 224
Green Tea and Baby Squid, page 225
Fennel, Vanilla, and White Chocolate, page 226

SUMMER

Malabar Spinach and Fish Tartare, page 227
New Zealand Spinach and Squid, page 228
Fish of the Day and Shiso, page 229
Dulse Seaweed and Cherries, page 230

FALL

Sage and Comté Cannelé, page 232
Oyster and Codium, page 232
Lamb Millefeuille, page 234
Mate and White Chocolate, page 235

WINTER

Oxalis and Crab, page 237
Red Belgian Endive and Bleu du Queyras Sauce, page 238
Radicchio Ravioli and Wild Boar Consommé, page 239
Chocolate and Rosemary, page 240

FLOWERS

SPRING

Rose Tuiles and Smoked Mackerel, page 242
Chrysanthemum Dome, Flaked Crab, and Spring Flowers, page 243
Petit Pois and Elderflower Ragout, page 244
Nasturtium Flower and Cucumber, page 245

SUMMER

Cosmos Veil and Veal Tartare, page 246
Sunflower Ravioli and Parmesan Bouillon, page 247
Zucchini Flower Ravioli and Chicken Consommé, page 248
Pollen, Honey, and Propolis, page 249

FALL

Hibiscus and Beet Rose, page 250
Lobster and Vanilla, page 251
Artichoke Tart, page 252
Yucca and Grapefruit, page 253

WINTER

Borage Flowers and Razor Clams, page 254
Osmanthus, Langoustine, and Green Apple, page 255
Saffron and Mussels, page 257
Violet and Unpasteurized Goat Milk, page 258

FRUITS

SPRING

Baby Fava Bean Tartlet and Pistachio, page 260
Caesar's Mushroom Tartar, page 261
Red and White Strawberries and Foie Gras, page 262
Taggiasca Olive and Lemon, page 263

SUMMER

Citrus bouillon, Snow Pea and Shrimp, page 265
Bell Pepper Tortellini and Octopus, page 266
Zucchini, Eggplant, and Tomato Tart, page 268
Raspberries and Verbena, page 269

FALL

Butternut Squash and Fish Tartare, page 270
Foie Gras and Porcini Mushrooms from the Col de Tende, page 271
Mallard and Quince Terrine, page 272
Prickly Pear and Yuzu, page 274

WINTER

Chia, Citron, and Venison Tartare, page 275
Fish of the Day and Sudachi Sauce, page 275
Squab and Banana from the Garden, page 276
Menton Lemon and Stracciatella, page 278

LIQUIDS

THE UNIVERSE OF LIQUIDS

Carefully created to enrich the dining experience with alternatives to alcoholic drinks, new pairings inspired by the four universes add to guests' pleasure and discovery at Mirazur.

A liquid universe with numerous variations, resulting from blends that are both innovative and captivating, made entirely at the restaurant using different ingredients.

Created to pair with each dish on the menu, the formulas combine a variety of flavors. They marry homemade fermented drinks such as kefir, kombucha, tepache, vinegar, and kavas with different infusions, decoctions, macerations, hydrolats, juices, extractions, pressings, and syrups.

The sommellerie and research teams are immersed in a new adventure and in-depth research—a work of precious alchemy—into the possibilities offered by fruits, vegetables, herbs, cereals, wild plants, and spices in their liquid form.

These artisanal and "living" drinks reflect our fascination with our environment and the protection of its biodiversity and enable us to come into contact with indigenous yeasts and bacteria that are involved in the various fermentation processes used.

DRINKS

ROOTS

SPRING

1. TAMARIND

Tamarind Paste
Pu'er Tea and Hibiscus Flower Infusion
Lingonberry Syrup

SUMMER

2. MENTON PINK ONION

Menton Pink Onion Infusion

AUTUMN

3. LICORICE

Licorice Kombucha
Cacao Peel and Black Pepper Infusion
Cherry Vinegar
Concentrated Tannins

WINTER

4. GINGER

Black Tea and Ginger Kombucha
Lemon Zest, Green Apple, and Red Bell Pepper Infusion
Peach Vinegar

LEAVES

SPRING

5. RHUBARB

Amaranth Leaf Infusion
Rose Vinegar
Marigold, Lavender, and Rhubarb Leaf Infusion
Blackcurrant Syrup

SUMMER

6. ROCK SAMPHIRE

Rock Samphire Kombucha
Citrus Fruit Syrup
Peach Vinegar

AUTUMN

7. VINE

Infusion of Vine, Linden, and Black Tea Leaves
Orange Plankton
White Wine Reduction
Yeasts
Cask-Flavored Water

WINTER

8. DULSE SEAWEED

Dulse Seaweed Kombucha
Homemade Caramel
Aniseed and Almond Infusion
Coffee

FLOWERS

SPRING

9. ELDERFLOWER

Lacto-Fermentation of Green Apple Peel and Sea Salt
Lemon Leaf Infusion
Elderflower Vinegar
Cider Vinegar

SUMMER

10. LAVENDER AND CHAMOMILE

Lavender, Chamomile, Osmanthus, and Hazelnut Infusion
Rose Kombucha
Pear and Tonka Bean Vinegar

AUTUMN

11. SAFFRON

Marigold Flower Mix
Saffron and Honey Infusion
Peach Vinegar
Apple Vinegar

WINTER

12. DRIED ROSE

Rose Petal and Amaranth Flower Infusion
Tannin Concentrate
Blueberry Vinegar

FRUITS

SPRING

13. ORANGE

Dried Orange, Hazelnut, Cypress Nut, and Juniper Decoction
Black Tea Infusion
Persimmon Vinegar

SUMMER

14. STRAWBERRY

Strawberry, Raspberry, and Toasted Red Peppercorn Infusion
Red Wine Reduction
Red Wine Vinegar

AUTUMN

15. PEAR

Pear Tepache
Chamomile Infusion

WINTER

16. HAZELNUT

Buckwheat Infusion
Hazelnut, Almond, and Vanilla Syrup
Green Apple and Goji Berry Tepache

1

2

3

4

5

6

7

8

9

10

11

12

13

14

15

16

MAURO COLAGRECO

The unique and unbounded culinary world that Mauro Colagreco has created is a testament to his passion and a career characterized by travel, discoveries, and conscientious work.

From his native Argentina to his move with his family to the Côte d'Azur, he has always sought to create a dining experience in harmony with the living world that surrounds us. His cuisine is rooted in a region and celebrates biodiversity, freedom, and the multiple influences that shape its creation.

Mirazur, which opened in 2006 in Menton, the last French village before Italy, has been attributed the supreme accolades of three Michelin stars and first place in the 2019 listing of The World's 50 Best Restaurants. The restaurant has also received a green star from the Michelin Guide for its environmentally responsible approach, as well as Plastic Free Certification: Mirazur is the first restaurant to have totally banished single-use plastic from its kitchens.

Colagreco is committed to questioning the notion of luxury and the role of gastronomy, with the aim of creating an intentional community and changing our habits to ensure better respect of life on our planet. A man who continues to pursue his dreams, Colagreco was recently appointed Unesco Goodwill Ambassador for Biodiversity, was elected vice president of the association Relais & Châteaux in recognition of his commitment to environmental responsibility.

PHOTOGRAPHER'S ACKNOWLEDGMENTS

Thank you to Luca, Paloma, Bianca, Chantal and Josef.

Matteo Carassale

Editorial department: Art de vie
Editorial director: Laure Aline
Editorial assistant: Marine Laurençot
Production: Titouan Roland
Graphic design and layout: Laurence Maillet

Translation: Anne McDowall
Proofreading: Nicole Foster
Still life design: Eleonora Turbiani
Ceramics on pages 163, 193, and 200: Odile Culas-Bonnin

Photo credit page 6: Marc Heller © Observatoire de la Côte d'Azur

195 Broadway
New York, NY 10007
abramsbooks.com

Connect with us at www.editionsdelamartiniere.fr
Instagram: @lamartiniere.cuisine

Photoengraving: IGS-CP
Legal deposit: November 2023
Printed and bound in August 2025 by Florjančič tisk. d.o.o.
Printed in Slovenia
ISBN : 978-1-4197-7423-2

ISBN 978-1-4197-7423-2
57500
9 781419 774232